# ENDORSEMENTS

*As a vegan . . . why would I read a book by a hunter? As an avid book lover and chaser of my dreams, I'm glad I moved past our differences and gave this book a chance. Amazingly I was drawn in—even by the hunting stories—where I have now learned to "turtle up" (and learned I am much braver around mice than Zech).*

*More than that, however, this is a beautiful Christian perspective on pushing ourselves beyond what we think we're capable of and realizing our own worth and impact on the world. Full of personal stories that are heartfelt and humorous, Zech packs a punch of real-life application and questions at the end of each chapter to keep you engaged and motivated to dig deep into your own life and dreams.*

*As a marriage and family coach, it's all about getting proactive in your home and being intentional about the family—and life—you dream of. This is a great read to start asking those questions and move you in the right direction.*

—Ashley Logsdon,
founder of Mama Says Namaste, marriage & family coach

*Zech has the kind of passion for life and his family we should all emulate. This book is laced with wisdom and unfiltered truth designed to help every driven entrepreneur find perspective and protect what matters most.*

—Seth Buechley,
author of *Ambition* and CEO of Cathedral Consulting

*Zech Newman's book* Chasing Dreams in a Minivan *is a unique addition to the entrepreneur's list of "must read" business books. He dares to weave faith, family, humor, and practical advice into this gem. Refreshingly honest, his advice is immediately applicable. Read* it with your spouse, and you will have plenty of future date night topics.

—Kathy Rushing,
relationship mentor for entrepreneur couples, KathyRushing.com

Chasing a dream is for those people who are ON FIRE with passion for freedom. If you want to succeed without losing your soul, Zechariah's heartfelt stories, goofy wisdom, and '90s pop culture references will keep you on the right road.

—John Lee Dumas,
host of *Entrepreneurs on Fire*

As someone who's been chasing his dreams for a long time, I found Zechariah's book to be a breath of fresh air. It made me think about my dream in a different way and how I might need to slow down to speed up. If you're stuck in a rut trying to move forward on your dreams, **Chasing Dreams in a Minivan** *is a great book to get you back on track and to achieve those goals. You'll come away feeling refreshed and inspired. You'll also have a plan for reaching those dreams.*

—Joe Lalonde,
author at JMLalonde.com

Too many people walk away from their dream swayed by those who say it's not possible or by circumstances that seem insurmountable. If you're one of those normal people, you'll hate this book. Using "uncommon" sense, humor, and profound insights, Zech shares how he went right straight toward his dream. This book will move you from "I wish" to "I did."

—Dan Miller,
New York Times bestselling author, *48 Days to the Work You Love*

Dreaming has always been a part of the fabric of my being. Whether it was watching Pinocchio and singing "When You Wish Upon a

*Star," cheering for the American Dream Dusty Rhodes as he would wrestle for the NWA heavyweight championship, or listening to "Dream On" by Aerosmith . . . I'm a dreamer. It took several years of adulthood to realize that no one will hand your dream to you, but you have to go out, have a plan, and intentionally pursue the dream. Zech is my buddy and fellow dreamer.*

*I wish I had this book ten years ago. I would have saved countless hours of hoping, and learned the practical steps for doing. I always liked the phrase "A,B,C . . . Action Brings Clarity." Zech breaks down fundamentals that will help you with clarity, purpose, and progress. This book is one of those that I will reread every so often to keep myself hungry and on track."*

—Jared Easley,
author and founder of Podcast Movement

*Can you laugh and learn at the same time? Can you follow another's journey and be inspired to live your own adventure? Yes and yes. This book will change your approach to life and relationships for the better!*

—Mike Loomis,
author, book coach, brand strategist at www.MikeLoomis.CO

*I have known this goofy, incredible, courageous, dream chaser for five years now, and on the days I felt most alone, Zechariah Newman has been there for me. When I questioned chasing my dream to serve fatherless fathers, Zech was there for me.*

*Now with* **Dream-Chasing in a Minivan***, I have all the wisdom, humor, and spiritual guidance I ever needed to become the father I was created to be, the man God wants me to be, and the son I always knew I could be, in one insightful book. This is one I will certainly read over and over again.*

*If you're a husband who loves his family and craves the life God promised you, this book is meant to cross your path. Go forth, find your dream, and chase it. Today. Because tomorrow may never come.*

—Jason Pockrandt,
author and speaker, www.fatherdaughterconversationsbook.com

*Zech Newman encourages readers to chase their dreams. But this isn't another Pollyanna self-help book full of unattainable tips. Instead, using wit and wisdom, Newman gives a practical guide to unleash the hopes that we've suppressed so we can start to live again.*

—David Rupert,
Patheos writer, speaker and author of
*Living a Life of Yes: One Word Changes Everything*

*Early on in this book, Zech writes, "If information doesn't move you to action, it's simply entertainment." When it comes to pursuing your dreams and goals, Zech's voice and approach are highly entertaining, so you'll stay engaged. But this book will also move you to action, which is the whole point of a book on pursuing your dreams. I'm known for the hashtag #DREAMtoDO, and if there ever was a #DREAMtoDO book, this is it!*

—Kent Julian,
speaker and author

# Chasing Dreams in a Minivan

## For Men with Big Goals and the Women Who Put up with Them

Zech Newman

**Chasing Dreams in a Minivan**
**For Men with Big Goals
and the Women Who Put Up with Them**
**Zech Newman**
Copyright © Zech Newman

All rights reserved.

ISBN: 9781728838083

No part of this book may be used or reproduced by any means, graphic, electronic, or mechanical, including photocopying, recording, taping or by any information storage retrieval system without the written permission of the author except in the case of brief quotations embodied in critical articles and reviews.

Cover design and editorial by MikeLoomis.CO

ZechariahNewman.com

# Dedication

Dedicated to the woman who saw something in a wide-eyed dreamer at seventeen years old. You have loved me at emo and at my best. Thank you for hearing me when I word-vomit about dreams and for believing in me when there was no evidence of potential. Rachel, I like you. I like you a lot.

To my kids Zoe, Luke, and Hope. May you chase after God, your spouse. kids (someday), and your dreams with a ferocious abandonment. Your daddy is proud of you and loves you more than he loves his dreams.

# Acknowledgements

I'd like to thank my wife, Rachel, who is the most merciful and grace-filled person I know. You had to endure two stages of this book: my failings—which produced the stories—and the process of my writing this book.

I am grateful for my mom. Mom, you gave birth to a legend. You were the first woman to ever believe in me. You helped me assimilate my thoughts and told me when my thoughts needed work. You have been my cheerleader when I doubted, and you constantly reminded me to lean on God and not my own understanding. Also, thanks to you, I will sell at least one copy of this book.

Dad, thank you for teaching me the art of adventure. I would be happy to get lost in the woods with you any day, even though you say, "Lost is a state of mind." Thank you for bringing this dreamer back to reality and to work. I know hard work because you showed me hard work. Also, I'm out of stories, and it's time to caribou hunt in the Yukon or chase elk in the Rockies.

I'm thankful for a brother who smiles at my crappy sense of humor. Reuben, you told me my ideas were awesome when they were terrible. You got mad at people who told me I couldn't do what I thought I could do. Thanks for giving me hope when I had none. Reuben, help me get Dad to go caribou hunting in the Yukon or elk hunting in the Rockies. We can fish, too.

My sister, Daniela. This book is (in a big way) thanks to you. You are the firstborn, a great leader, and a go-getter. You are the great communicator in the family, and I have spent a lifetime trying to catch up to you. Thanks for reminding me who I am many times when I doubted. You cast a big shadow, and I hope I make you proud.

To the editor who has become a friend: Mike Loomis is a magician, (unless you hate this book, then he is awful.) He had patience with me through the process and delays. He cared first, edited second, and believed in me enough for me to get over my fears and use my cheesy humor. Thank you for enhancing my voice and not trying to change it. You are a legend, sir.

# Contents

Introduction ………………………………………………………..… 1
Chapter 1: The forest …………………………………………….... 5
Chapter 2: Desert ..…………………………………………………13
Chapter 3: Secret Sauce …………………………………………..19
Chapter 4: Where Art Thou, Big Papa? …………………….….. 25
Chapter 5: Lava Fields ..…………………………………………. 31
Chapter 6: You Suck, I Suck, We all Suck …………………….. 39
Chapter 7: Flossing to a Dream ………………………………..49
Chapter 8: False Summits ……………………………………… 55
Chapter 9: Stinky Fish …………………………………………..63
Chapter 10: Lone Wolf …………………………………………..71
Chapter 11: United We Stand ..…………………………………79
Chapter 12: Communication ..………………………………….87
Chapter 13: Hideaway Beach ..…………………………………95
Chapter 14: A True Warrior ……………………………….....103
Chapter 15: Future Past ..……………………………………….111
Chapter 16: Write Your Own (Short) Book ………………..117

# Introduction

Every one of us has a dream for our destiny and calling. Deep inside each of us is a cry for our purpose, which reveals our place in this world. Our dreams all look different, but mine went something like this . . .

I was walking on a cold, dreary day with the Oregon rain falling on my face, when out of nowhere a light pierced the darkness and a host of angels began to sing, "Welcome to the Jungle."

From the light, a voice like Morgan Freeman's boomed, "This is Zechariah Newman . . . and he's here to save the world!" This voice went on to detail exactly what I was to do and how long I'd have to work. And yes, the angels were still singing.

This revelation obviously transformed my life. I was to travel the world, work four hours a week, help millions of people, and make millions of dollars. A win–win for humanity—and me. I would be a cross between Mother Teresa and Richard Branson.

Maybe your dreams don't include angels, 1980s classic rock, or a voice like Morgan Freeman. Okay, they probably don't include any of those things. However, there is one thing universal to dreamers: the great tension between reality and our dreams. (Come to think of it, maybe Morgan Freeman would read the audio version of this book . . .)

What we've dreamed up in the spaces between our ears and beating in our chest can make us go emo because reality and our dream are often miles apart.

Depressed and disillusioned, we can give up our dream of living a purposeful life.

Not only do we carry this tension when today's reality and our dream don't match, but life often punches us in the face along the way.

The great philosopher Mike Tyson was right when he said, "Everyone has a plan until they get punched in the face." (Mr. Tyson is not on my audiobook narrators list, by the way. No offense, Mike.) The punches come in many forms, like when you need support, but a loved one doesn't understand your dream. So, rejection hits you in the gut, and a lack of progress beats you down.

Make it through the punches, and you have the hurdle of being present with your family and others you love. You know that little word called "balance."

Balance often feels like a rainbow you're trying to touch, but it is always a little out of reach. You'll have to pull back on your dream when it's inconvenient and push through when you'd rather hang out with friends. Balancing the tightrope of vision and presence is about as hard as it looks in the circus, except there's no safety net.

I know this might not seem like an uplifting introduction, but there's hope for you. How do I know?

I'm now living my dream.

No, not the Morgan Freeman dream, but the real dream I had for my life that was buried under the rubble of the super-lame dream I described.

Don't worry, this isn't one of those "my life used to suck, now it's awesome books." In this book, we'll look into some practical steps to unearth dreams that bring life. I'll point out some guidelines to make the journey a little easier. You'll discover how to run a race that honors God and brings your family into your dream.

Although you've figured out that I enjoy quirky humor (and by "quirky" I mean not funny to most people), this book was written through pain and through joy. It is the guidebook for chasing Godly dreams with your family.

You can achieve your dream by changing the way you think, the way you work, and the way you deal with your full plate of responsibilities. With God, all things are possible.

As you'll soon discover, I learned a lot the hard way. I wish I would have had some guidelines and guardrails on my journey—or at least listened to my wife more. My hope is that you can be spared some of those experiences. So, in each chapter, I'll ask you a few questions and lead you in a process to write out a sentence or two to help create your own guidelines and guardrails, as well as a prayer to consider.

Don't skip those opportunities to write and pray, okay? This journey of chasing a dream is a mental, emotional, physical, and spiritual one.

At the end of the book, we'll put them together into a magical piece of paper you can take to the bank and exchange for gold bars . . . or something even better and easier to carry.

So buckle up, play, "Welcome to the Jungle," and let's dive into making an impact on this world.

# Chapter 1

## The Forest

When you're lost in the woods with someone and the sun is setting, it's important to keep up your manly persona and not let anyone know you're freaking out.

My dad and I were hunting in the Oregon mountains. If you're vegan, don't worry, no animals were harmed in the telling of this story. Harming happens in another hunting story later in the book. By the way, I'm a bad hunter.

When we left that morning, we planned to spend the night in the back country of the Cascades, on a ridge we'd hunted on many times before. However, as the sun was setting, we found ourselves lost in a dense growth area of pine, and we couldn't see more than a foot in front of our faces.

Confused and disoriented, we could've been walking in circles, but as darkness sank in around us, the trees finally broke open to a small meadow. With our head lamps on, we started a fire and laid down our sleeping bags, on what I'm pretty sure was the lumpiest area on the entire ridge.

As we tried to sleep, sets of eyes watched us from the edge of the meadow, and mice scurried all over our sleeping bags. I may or may not have rolled closer to my dad—you know, for his protection. That's just the type of guy I am.

Needless to say, I didn't sleep much that night.

When you don't know where you are, fear takes over and causes the eyes glowing in the woods to turn into bloodthirsty zombies. My dad said they were coyotes, but they were zombies—

zombies that would attack as soon as I fell asleep. I pretty much saved our lives with all my worrying. *You're welcome, Dad.*

The next morning eventually arrived. We broke camp and kept our compasses out to make sure we stayed consistent in one direction. After an hour of hiking through the brush, we finally reached a clearing. We retrieved our maps and checked the topography to discover we weren't as far off course as we'd thought. With only a minor adjustment, we were back on track.

The first test any dream chaser has to overcome is the forest test.

Trying to figure out if you're on track with your dream is like being lost in a forest.

In many ways, we believe we have a clear picture of where we're headed. Similar to the great awakening, I imagined in the beginning. However, dream-chasing is often murkier. If you're waiting for your dream to be clear before you move in a certain direction, you'll find yourself lost in the woods—or you'll never leave home. You'll be zombie food before you ever reach your dream.

Usually, our journey and path aren't clear until we look back. We often end up somewhere different than we intended in the beginning. The journey through the forest can prepare us for better adventures—if we let it. And it can be fun, especially if we push past the fear.

Fear turns coyotes into zombies and mice crawling on your sleeping bags into, well . . . mice crawling on your sleeping bag. It's just creepy; mice are pretty much Satan's best friend. Never trust someone who likes mice. That's a bonus tip for you; your investment in this book is paying off already.

Fear lives, breathes, and grows in the shadowy places of our minds. Fear is defeated in the light. When we're fearful, taking our fear into the light is the last thing we want to do. We want to keep our "man card" and not appear afraid. We believe the lie that fear whispers in our ear. We sit and wait for the zombies to eat our face instead of shining a flashlight into the glowing eyes to find a small coyote. We lie to those around us and say we didn't really want the dream anyway.

Lying about our desires, or denying the reality of fear, can leave us as half the man we used to be.

Though defeating fear isn't as easy as using a flashlight, it's really not difficult. Often fear is healthy because fear points to risk. There are ways to mitigate risk, and we'll talk about those as this book unfolds. However, in order to reduce fear, I use a simple three-part process: say it, replace it, and turtle up.

Speaking your fear to someone else is scary. I know what you may be thinking: *You want me to reduce fear by doing something else that's risky and causes fear?* Simple idea, but not easy. Most of us try the John Wayne method of riding off into the sunset alone. Facing fear on our own seems less risky, but it's actually the opposite. The habit of running with people in the same direction as you're running and communicating your fear to them will reduce the fear to a realistic risk level. Remember, fear points to risk, but is your risk a coyote or a zombie? It's important to know the difference. Speak out your fear to reduce risk to what it actually is.

Replace your fear with truth that's greater than you. Empty space in your mind is still a place, and if you just say, "I'm not going to fear," you'll fail to defeat your foe. When we fail to *replace* our fear with truth, we're like a toddler who covers their eyes and thinks no one can see them. Cute for a kid, but we look ridiculous behaving like this as an adult. It's like wearing one of those Forever Lazy outfits. (If you own one, I have no words. You probably like mice too. In fact, that's something you should confess for other reasons.)

Truth, which I accept above fear, and above my own feelings, is from the Bible. So, when I'm struggling with a specific fear, I memorize a passage of scripture. For example, when I was in the woods afraid of having my face removed by the zombies, I recited, "For God did not give us a spirit of fear but of power and love and self-control."

Another truth to accept, to replace the exaggerations and lies in the shadows of your mind, is truth from the friends with whom you shared your fear. Just like my dad helped me in the forest by sharing the truth of what the glowing eyes really were, your friends can speak truth into fears you've overblown—if you have a high trust level and you'll believe what they tell you.

I may or may not have said this to myself about a million times that night: "Those eyes are just small dogs."

Fear is reduced to its smallest form when we "turtle up." No, I'm not talking about the Ninja Turtles; though as a kid I dreamed I'd someday write about those awesome pizza-loving ninjas.

Turtle up means to take small, slow, consistent steps.

When I began writing, I took small steps because I was concerned about what others would think of me. First, I wrote where no one would see my words. Then, I started a blog where no one would know it was me. Finally, I told people I had a blog and set up an author page. I was scared the whole time, including being scared as I wrote this sentence.

This book is scary for me to write because I'm finally writing in a voice that's 100% me. *What if other Christians don't like zombies, ACDC, and hunting? Worse yet, what if they like mice and the Forever Lazy? What if they are vegan?*

Just a few thoughts that have gone through my mind. Yeah, it's weird up there.

Fear won't be 100% forgotten when you take an action step toward your dream. If you haven't told anyone what you have been dreaming about, start there. If you *have* told people but are putting off action, take one small step to begin. Fear might be more manageable when you make progress and score wins, but you'll need to decide to move toward your dream *in spite of* your fear.

But don't leap too quickly and overrun what your fear tolerance can handle. Turtle up.

Conquering fear is a momentum game. Eventually the fear will reduce to the level where you barely know it exists. Start small, turtle up, and yell a "cowabunga!" or two if you're feeling really sassy. Whatever it takes to begin to face realistic risk.

Dream chasers have a tendency to wait, watching webinars or subscribing to emails from online superheroes, instead of moving forward toward our dream. We consume more information and read more blogs. The information age has us lost in the woods, and the worst part is we don't even know it. We can fall in love with information.

If information doesn't move you into action, it's simply entertainment. I have no problem with entertainment, but we must be honest: is the information we're consuming is simply entertainment, or is it helping to move our dream forward?

Action is required to reach your dream. Action is required to move us out of the forest. Years from now, you'll wish you'd taken a chance—a turtle-sized step. Then another.

Movement without direction is like chasing your tail. To help us get out of the woods, my father and I used a compass. We walked in the same direction for a long time. Even though we didn't know our exact location, we knew west and east would eventually lead us to either side of the ridge, and we'd be able to see. So, we moved west and only west.

We still *felt* lost, but in reality, we were becoming less lost with every step.

When first chasing your dream, you're unsure if you can really achieve what's in your heart. The only way to combat uncertainty is to move in one direction for a predetermined period of time. Momentum happens when we stay consistent.

We don't work out at the gym for one week and expect raging six-pack abs. Trust me. I've tried! Instead of looking like Arnold after my one week at the gym, I looked like myself—only more tired. It was a sad week, but I've moved on.

Move in a consistent direction to make it out of the woods and into the open. Brief moments of clarity appear, and then disappear, as you move toward the next layer of your dream. We like to believe our dreams are "destinational" when the reality is most of us reach our dream and then have a new dream. (By the way, *destinational* isn't a real word, and isn't part of a real dream.) We are designed by God to dream. Dreaming doesn't cease until we are six feet under.

Some of us get lost in the woods, while others stop on the ridge of clarity. Don't settle.

Stopping on the ridge of clarity is like taking up settlement in a location we weren't designed to live. It may feel comfortable for a short time, but the reality is, life is in constant motion. We are either advancing forward or stuck in the comfortable and falling behind.

Continue to push through and find comfort in the uncomfortable unknown. Change of mindsets and forward movement lead us to prosperity in the forest.

## Guidelines and Guardrails:

What makes you the most fearful when you think about your dream?
_____
_____

Who can you confide in?
_____
_____

What is one small action that will overcome this fear?_____
_____

When I am feeling fearful about _____, I will tell _____, who will give me the courage to_____
_____

## Prayer:

*Dear God, I confess that too often I am controlled by fear. I choose today to not live in my fear any longer but move in spite of my fear. Give me the courage to move forward and the wisdom to know what I should do. Amen.*

# Chapter 2

# Desert

I'd been hunting antelope in Eastern Oregon for several days and had come up short on several close encounters. No, I don't look for hunting illustrations, they just find me—more often than I find antelope!

One morning, during my hunting trip, my dad and brother slept in, but I wanted to be in prime antelope-viewing position before sunrise. I hiked a couple of hours from camp to a bluff where I'd have a view of the valley. As the sun began to rise, I saw a flash in the distance.

I raised my binoculars and spotted thirty antelope. I decided to make a stalk on them, so I headed east toward the heard. After a couple of hours, I was within seven hundred yards. I began to crawl so I'd be close enough for a shot.

Finally, I closed the gap to a distance I felt comfortable shooting and slowly pulled the trigger. My shot hit its mark, and I bagged an antelope. As I processed the animal, the summer sun began to beat down. The last few days, temperatures soared into the nineties, and this day felt no different. With no shade, I worked until I could fit all the meat in my pack and make one trip out. I retrieved my compass and headed west toward camp.

I had less water then I would've liked, but just enough for the trip back to camp. Mile after mile, the journey seemed to take longer than I thought it would. *Maybe it just felt longer because of the extra weight on my back.*

Three hours into the hike, I stopped and sat under a scrawny juniper tree and drank my last drops of water. I tried to reach my dad and brother on my CB radio. I should've been back to camp by then, and nothing around me looked familiar. It didn't make sense. I sat and weighed my options and started to get nervous. (I know, from the earlier story, you realize I have nerves of steel. Or steel wool.)

I stood up and continued west. I remembered there was a gravel road that ran north and south and hoped I'd eventually run into it. After more miles, I found another juniper tree to sit under. My throat began to close, and I began to see stars. I was in the full effects of dehydration and couldn't go much farther.

I tried using the CB again and prayed my dad and brother would answer. After about thirty minutes, I received a faint reply back. A few minutes later, I heard nothing. After what felt like an eternity, I heard them again, and with every reply, their voices became clearer.

After a few minutes, they drove right by me. I was only a quarter mile from the gravel road. They turned around, helped me load up the antelope, and gave me plenty of water to drink. That water tasted like pure manna from heaven (and was certainly on my gratitude list that day.)

As we drove back to camp, my father told me I had ended up north of camp by several miles. Really, I don't get lost every time I go hunting. I usually have the directional instinct of a migrating duck, I tell you.

Every dreamer has to survive, and hopefully thrive, in the desert.

The desert reveals very few signs of life, so it's easy to get lost on the way to your dreams. In other words, we need an internal confidence to guide us when appearances seem lifeless.

I made a couple of key mistakes on that hunting trip. My favorite mistake was when I found out I'd shot my antelope within three hundred yards of a road I could've driven to. (*Did you just laugh at me?*) Three hundred freaking yards from where I started. I could've sat there, enjoyed a margarita, and worked on my tan instead of almost killing myself.

Another key mistake was that I didn't slow down and look around. When you're in the desert, it can be tempting to sprint. However, as you sprint, you can lose orientation and cost yourself more time. Coach John Wooden had a great saying: "Be quick, but don't hurry."

Slow down and weigh your actions. I'm ADD but supercharged when it comes to hiking and dream-chasing. I have a tendency to move in a zigzag pattern, wasting energy and time. My hurrying can send me miles out of the way instead of noticing the small four-wheel-tracked road right next to me. I work really hard to outwork my stupidity.

How about you? What are your tendencies as you pursue your dream? Are you an ultra planner, or are you so bent on action that you don't think?

Think through your actions. While in the desert, where there are few signs of life, you'll have to stick to your plan without seeing results. The lack of results can make anyone want to give up on their dream. Yet some even try to outwork their environment. Resist this temptation and slow down. You'll move farther faster if you come up with a solid plan.

As you make your "turtle up" plan to drive through fear, you also need to figure out ways to measure progress. Lag measurements are results that take longer to see—and in the desert can be highly discouraging. Lead measurements are tangible things that you can see today to show you life in the desert.

For example, I'm trying to lose ten pounds right now. The weight is the lag measurement. The lead measurement is the action I take (or don't take). I am intermittently fasting daily. I am working out six days a week. I am abstaining from alcohol and eating out. All of these actions are measurable, and I can see life before result.

What can you measure to give you signs of life?

Make sure you're trying to solve the *right* problem. I attempted, and eventually succeeded, in heading back toward camp in one trip. But that was the wrong goal. My goal should've been focused on the easiest way to get myself and my animal back to camp. If that would've been my goal, creativity would've been my ally. Instead I relied on brute strength and stubborn willpower.

Stop trying to muscle your way to your goals. I know you're yoked out of your mind, but you're no Arnold. How can we think about our objectives differently?

Take some time, write down your current goal, and then think about how you can tweak it to discover your four-wheel drive shortcut road. Most likely, there's a more efficient way to reach your goal then you currently realize. Not only do you need to slow down on your journey in order to speed up, you also need a map. The morning I raced out of camp, I left my map on the table. A compass is great for knowing the direction you're headed, but you also need to know where you are and where you're headed.

A map would've shown me to head southwest and would've shown me I wasn't in route to where I wanted to be. A map shows you where you are and where you need to go. I know that was mind-blowing information about maps, but often it's the simplest things we overlook when we're chasing a dream in our hearts.

As dream chasers, we either struggle with *where* we want to go because the picture is fuzzy, or we're not brutally realistic about where we *are*. Clarity on both ends of the spectrum creates the best route to your dreams. This tension isn't fun, and it made me depressed the first time I really looked at my situation. My depressive feeling was worth it; reality checks move us closer to our dreams even though it feels like the opposite.

Disillusionment sounds terrible, but it's actually the destruction of an *illusion*. Disillusionment means you're one critical step in the journey from turning your dream into a reality.

Disillusionment is only possible when we know where we are and how far we have to go.

The journey to reaching our dream takes much longer then you or I would like. Our unrealistic time frame has us crying for our momma under a juniper tree—figuratively speaking, of course.

We must gain information and skill and hone our craft—and it doesn't happen overnight. The more unfamiliar you are with the craft required to reach your dream, the longer the road ahead. There are shortcuts, but nothing will overcome the need for practice and growth.

Starting with the end in mind clears up the destination, but where are you on the journey? What are your weaknesses? What skills do you need to develop? How will you be different from your competition? Ask honest, introspective questions to help develop a proper map. If you don't know what skill to work on, ask those around you for their feedback. Being brutally honest about where you are and hopeful about your future is necessary to get through the desert.

Another necessity is hope. Hope is fuel to your soul.

When our illusion is stripped away, there can be a void in our heart. That's why we replace illusion with hope. When we lose hope, we lose our desire to move forward. Look at your journey with a fresh perspective. Have hope that the plan you created can be accomplished. Measure your lead wins to increase your hope meter. One hot, dehydrated step at a time.

## Guidelines and Guardrails:

How far from your dream are you?

_____

_____

What are some lead measurements you can have that will show you progress?

_____

_____

Where can you apply creativity instead of using brute force?

_____

_____

Looking at my dream, I realize that I am (how far) _____ away. I will measure my traction by measuring _____. My eyes and mind will be on the lookout for creative solutions.

## Prayer:

*Dear God, honestly, the desert is so discouraging. I admit my lack of faith and choose to trust You. Thank You for giving me a mind that is able to come up with creative solutions. Guide me into figuring out some lead measurements to increase my hope. I thank You in advance. Amen.*

# Chapter 3

## Secret Sauce

Punching someone in the face when they're not expecting it is a great way to protect yourself.

This was my life motto as a fourteen-year-old boy who just switched schools. Don't take this advice. I was in about eight fights that year and earned the nickname, "Rocky." Not my proudest moment. Honestly, I was scared and scarred.

Two years earlier, when I was twelve years old, the most miraculous thing happened. I, all of a sudden, knew everything. And another equally amazing miracle happened: my father, once wise and smart, suddenly knew nothing. I think every youngster goes through this phase, but for me, I was fortunate to have someone around I would listen to.

One of the youth leaders at my church earned my respect and captured my ear. He was a mountain of a man, standing over six feet tall. I wanted to be just like him. Our small group fed the homeless together. We played paintball and went to the beach. It was such an exciting time because I was growing closer to God and closer to a community.

This church group was like a family. I trusted them with my heart, and I believe they trusted me.

One morning, I walked into my youth group meeting and the tension in the room was so overwhelming you could cut it with a spoon. My youth leader was nowhere to be found. Instead, there was a police officer standing in the front of the room. I'm not the most observant person in the world, but having a police officer in the room isn't a good sign that things are normal. I asked one of my youth leaders what was going on. He said, "I'll explain in a minute. Please have a seat." Another bad sign.

He went on to explain to the group that the youth leader I looked up to, that I'd trusted my heart to, that I wanted to emulate, had turned himself in to the police. He had confessed to inappropriately touching some young boys in his past. I was devastated.

We were told we could no longer talk with him, even when he was released from jail. My heart hardened that day. I thought I'd learned something that day: you can't trust people.

The next year, I happened to move into private school. While making new friends, I stayed distant and didn't allow people in to my heart. It was a year of self-imposed solitary confinement. Ah, the joys of switching schools right after being wounded. But I wouldn't risk my heart again.

The next year, I switched back to public school, and it was much larger than the private school I attended the year before. Switching schools three times in three years was not awesome for creating friendships.

Someone picked a fight with me, so I punched him square in the face. I liked the power that came with beating someone up. I liked hurting them before they hurt me. (Remember that if you're considering a negative Amazon review of my book.)

That's where the stupid mantra, "Punch someone in the face before they have a chance to hurt you," came from. It really helped my loneliness.

I stopped fighting after that year, but I didn't stop hiding. I tried to hide from others in so many ways like drinking alcohol, viewing pornography, playing sports, and establishing a false religious persona.

The more I hid my true self, the more I hated myself. I didn't like myself, so I pretended to be someone else. I was afraid to talk, and I hated that about myself. I wished I were bold and courageous. I lived as someone else in my imagination.

My vices became a place to hide and stole more from me than I could have imagined. It wasn't until I was in my thirties that I could admit any struggles. It wasn't until I was in my thirties that I allowed myself to be healed from self-hatred. My ways of hiding were a form of protection that caged me.

I didn't realize it at the time, but I'd applied a mask to my life—a really stupid mask. We all tend to wear masks of some kind. No not super cool superhero masks like Deadpool or Batman, but stupid zombie masks.

The world hurts us, and our masks promise to shield us from the pain of this world. You may not go with the tough-guy routine, but your mask, whichever one you choose, leads to death. The mask may promise to protect us, but it actually leads us to the death of who God created us to be.

The mask prevents us from being loved and accepted, transforming us into a lifeless void. When we show the world a false version of ourselves, we know they don't and can't love the true version. They only love the version we allow them to see. And we question if they'll love what's behind the mask at all.

The Bible says we can love because He first loved us. That's a great promise, but here's the problem. When we don't allow even God into the dark places of our hearts, we can't receive love and therefore can't give love to the fullness that God intended.

What has love got to do (got to do) with it? Everything!

Love is the foundation of life itself. Love is pervasive and overwhelming. Our identity in Christ is what frees us to walk into our calling, and it's only known when we allow love in. Don't believe the lie like I did for so many years. I believed that what I was pretending to be was better than who God made me to be.

When we strive to become something that's already been given to us by God, we take energy from where it should be allocated. We become hiders instead of creators. We become fearful instead of people of faith. We become consumed with the outside circumstances instead of the inside, where change actually happens. We waste precious energy that could be used for chasing a dream.

If we try to figure out and pursue our dream without removing our masks, we focus on areas outside our responsibility. We'll either chase the wrong dream, or it will take longer to reach our dream.

Pursuing a dream while wearing a mask is a surefire way to become miserable.

We become consumed with what others think when we wear a mask. The more we understand our identity in Christ, the less we care what other people do or say. The less we care about what other people do or say, more gold within us is discovered. Gold is inside you now, so don't cover it up with a pertinacious mask.

Mask removal is pretty easy; you simply risk everything.

That's how it feels at first, allowing God and others into spaces you haven't allowed anyone before. It feels like jumping out of a plane without a parachute. Easy advice is often hard to follow. The mask will always be a temptation to apply because it feels easier. Most dependencies feel easier in the moment.

To remove the mask, we need to know, really know, that when we allow Christ to invade our heart, we have complete wholeness and meaning. What often happens in this process is we fall down, see ourselves as failures, and then fail some more. We need to remember what the Bible says about our identity. In Christ, we are complete. Nothing can separate us from the love of God. We are salt and light in the earth. Pretty much, you are a big deal. You are God's handiwork.

We can be fully honest with God about our struggles. Sadly, God, the creator of the universe, is often the last one we pour out our heart to. But when we open fully to God, even when we're angry with Him or we're struggling to do what He wants, we can feel the amazing way He loves us.

If you've never looked at the psalms David wrote and sang, do so. They can give you the courage to be real to God about your pain.

For me, it sounds like this, "God why are you doing this to me?! I want to serve you with all of my heart and mind, yet the things that I believe you placed in my heart aren't happening! What a cruel joke to give me desires that I can't reach. I am ticked off at you. Why? I just don't get it. I trust you, but I'm really struggling to trust you. I know you love me, but I'm really struggling to see that you love me. Please show me your love today and expand my heart and mind to trust you more."

When we tell God our most vulnerable thoughts and feelings, He doesn't run away. In fact, New Testament guy, James, wrote this: "Draw near to God and He will draw near to you." Receiving God's love is the first step to truly being able to love others. First John 4:19 says, "We love because he first loved us." Allow God into your shame and fear. Allow God into your struggle in faith and love. Allow God into all of you. He can handle it. He is God, you know.

God wired us for relationship with Him and for relationship with others. Being real with God is essential. And we must be real with trustworthy people. We're looking for complete freedom, and that requires us to have a band of believers around us. We must have a small group of people we can be honest with. It's not easy.

I remember the first time I admitted a sin I'd been holding on to for a long time. I nearly wet my pants in fear. Nearly. If I had, do you think I'd write about it?

Being honest with people who can love us is a crucial step to becoming who we are meant to be. By knowing our royal identity in Christ, confessing our crap to God and man, we can remove our masks and walk in authority. We must build into our lives the habit of talking with God and others. We must build in confession. It's a cleansing of our mind, heart, and soul.

As we remove our masks and walk as our true selves, new dreams will appear, and old dreams we've allowed to run by the wayside will pop up. We'll be free to pursue them.

We're loved, struggles and all.

Choose to act now. Pray to God, or call a friend you trust. Get the burden off your chest and allow love in.

## Guidelines and Guardrails:

Who can you sit down and talk with?

_____

_____

What things are you tempted to hide from others?

_____

_____

Do you feel like you're pursuing your true dream?

_____

_____

I am often tempted to hide _____ when I am _____. I will talk and confess this to _____ so that I can feel free to chase my dream.

## Prayer:

*Dear God, I confess that I hide things from You and others. I'm done hiding, and I confess _____ (list sins and false beliefs). God, I walk forward in freedom and know that You love me. Please show me Your love so that I can love myself and others more. I want to serve You as my true self and not the masked, fake version. Amen.*

# Chapter 4

## Where Art Thou, Big Papa?

As I parked in the driveway, I began to pull myself together. I wiped the tears from my face and took a deep breath. That's how I've been driving home lately.

My wife and I had lost our fourth baby due to a miscarriage, and I was uncertain if fatherhood was in the cards.

All I wanted was to be a dad. All my wife wanted was to be a mom.

I'd just gotten the news at work that another teenager who worked for me was pregnant and was debating whether to get an abortion or not. In that moment in time, I was pissed off at God, and I let him know it.

Drive after drive, I would pour my heart out to God, and for two years, He was silent. I didn't understand why God would hold back from me, yet people who didn't want children were having them. It wasn't fair.

Our view of God and his involvement in our dream is crucial to our dream-chasing journey and to life itself.

My attitude during this heartbreaking time went something like this. First, I entered into the mode of letting God, the creator of time and space, know, "I got this." I told Him that I know better than He does. He can stay in His church box and out of my business.

The more I allowed my wounding to control my thoughts and actions, the more I'd protect myself by trying to control my life. But it was more an appearance of control.

What areas are you trying to control that you have no real control over?

I couldn't control if my wife and I had a baby or not. We must remind ourselves that we don't have control over everything. That can be really scary when we have been under the illusion of supreme control. We must focus on doing our part in our dream and allow God to do His. We must hand over the controls.

The more we admit our inability without God, the more powerful and unstoppable we become.

When I dried my crying eyes and went in the house to be the strong man for my wife, she was crying. She was crying with joy. She told me she'd been praying and really felt like we should prepare for a baby.

That was probably the worst idea I'd ever heard. But I was wise enough to hold my tongue and ask, "Okay, how should we prepare?"

"I have paint, and I think we should paint the room," she said.

So, we painted the room.

As that roller went up and down the wall, we wept. Not the angry, *I'm pissed off at God, and I got this* tears. But the *I don't get this, God, and I don't know what to do* tears.

When we aren't living a life we envision, it leads us into a skewed perspective. We fixate on two periods of time: the past and the future.

It's pretty easy to focus on our past failures. I like to beat myself up a little more just to prove I'm remorseful. We relive the mistakes over and over and think about how we could've handled situations differently. What's worse is we start telling ourselves that God is somehow punishing us for something we've done. We look in the rearview mirror and don't think about anything else.

The other place we like to live in is the future. I live there a lot. You can obsess over your future and how great it will be, or you may obsess over the dangers lurking ahead. We can become so obsessed with the future that we forget to do anything today.

That's how I was thinking about my empty arms waiting on a baby. Until I painted the room.

Painting helped me return to the present instead of obsessing about what I didn't know. We focused on what we could do in the day. It gave me hope, but also it gave me action.

In everything, we should be focused on what we should do—in the here and now.

Instead of obsessing over what may come, we should stop, close our eyes, and take a deep breath. *God, what do you want me to do now?*

Our "now" may be taking a nap, writing down ideas, playing with the kids, or meeting someone for lunch. Being present in the moment is a requirement, not an option.

We are so drawn to other places besides the now, checked-out in dread or fantasy. We don't need to know what life will be like in twenty years, but we want to know because we're control freaks. Twenty years from now won't help you today. Only working on what's next can help our today.

Only in "next mode" can we make the life we want later.

As I painted the room with my wife, something broke, and it wasn't my aching back. What broke was my realization that I didn't trust God. Lack of trust was the crux of all my fighting—internally and externally—with Him.

When we don't fully trust God, we don't give over our whole life to Him. When we don't trust God, we put on the mask to Him and others. When we don't trust Him, we start to obsess over our future, or our past. Anxiety and fear become our bondage.

With Christ, we have peace, love, joy, patience, kindness, goodness, self-control, and awesomeness. Okay, maybe not awesomeness, but everything else. If those characteristics aren't present, at some level, something is wrong.

I'm happy to say that a couple of months later, my wife was pregnant again.

Every time we passed by that room, we stood in hope. When we walked by, we were reminded that God is in control and that all things, even the really sucky things, would work for the good of those that are called according to His purpose. We needed that reminder.

Zoe was the name of our first child, and we wept a whole different type of tear the day she was born. Her name means life, because we found another measure of life while painting her room. We now have three wonderful kids. Prayers, and tears, answered.

I now cry about other wants to God.

The tension between where we are and what we want life to look like will always be there. (Isn't that warm and fuzzy? I feel like the motivational guru. Maybe I'll put that on a poster.) But here's that reality memo once again. You'll never get to the point where you don't have to trust God in the tension that exists between your reality and what you want.

Only as we submit to God can we be a dreamer who pursues their calling in a healthy way. Because His ways won't make sense to our minds sometimes.

When we lay down what seems to promise control but actually brings bondage, we find peace and vision. While trying to become master, we make ourselves slave. We can't chase our dreams from bondage, only in freedom. Freedom is won by surrendering to Christ.

In Christ, we are righteous and royalty. Royal people chase royal dreams.

If you trust Him and do what you can with what you have, He will take you places you could never imagine.

God is here. He speaks. Will you listen? Listen now.

## Guidelines and Guardrails:

Do you tend to focus more on the past or the future?

_____

_____

Which part of the past or future do you fixate on?

_____

_____

What is one action that you can take to focus you on the present?

_____

_____

When I focus on over my (past/future), I'm tempted to fixate on _____, which is outside of my control. Instead I will_____ without delay.

## Prayer:

*Dear God, I confess that often I am filled with regret about my past and fear about the future. Forgive me for focusing on what You can redeem. Instead of fear and regret, I will walk forward in faith that Your plans for my life are better than my own. I will do what I can do and trust You to do what You do. Amen.*

# Chapter 5

# Lava Fields

"Don't touch that, or your leg will burn off!" my brother shouted. My left leg hung precariously close to the molten lava below. I slowly regained my footing and stood up, narrowly avoiding a fiery fate.

I quickly jumped from blackened rock to blackened rock. I could almost feel the volcanic steam rise up as the beads of sweat ran down my face. Finally, I stopped on a ledge to catch my breath and think. *How am I going to get out of this one?*

My family was counting on me, their eldest son, for rescue. As I looked around, I saw no other way to get to reach the other side of the gaping chasm. There was only one option. I must construct some sort of bridge to reach the next rock. Doing my best MacGyver imitation, I constructed a crude platform—and hoped it would hold my weight.

After several precarious steps onto the shaky bridge, I realized I was in deep trouble. I couldn't turn back, and I didn't know if I could move forward. I began to lose my balance, so I decided it was time for a backup plan.

I screamed for my brother, Reuben. "Help!"

He, like a typical younger brother, took his sweet time to save me. "Will you hurry up, I'm going to die!"

"I have to feed my pet dragon first!" he yelled.

"What?" I responded in surprise. "Dragons aren't real! Come back to reality and save me!" My brother always ruins everything with his nonconformity, while some of us have real work to do.

Sadly, and suddenly, I slipped into the lava and died a terrible but quick death. *Thanks a lot, Reuben. Always late to save me, and now my demise is on your hands. Live with that, buddy.*

If you've never played "hot lava" as a kid, you missed out. Your living room suddenly transforms from a boring couch, coffee table, and chairs into a menacing set of boulders—and the carpet becomes a sizzling sea of molten lava. Hours of riveting entertainment can be had with a little imagination.

Games like this remind me we're all born to be visionaries. To "see" what can't yet be seen. No one has to teach a child to use their imagination; it's as natural as breathing.

Made in the image of God the creator, we are born to create something out of nothing. We are all designed to create, yet many of us drift away from creating into living according to accepted norms—also known as "reality."

We give up lava fields, secret languages, and monster-slaying for forty-hour work weeks, status symbols, debt, and people-pleasing. We move from being rebel world changers on the fringe to respectable channel changers on the couch. And we lose the art of vision.

We often accept rules to this life that were made up by other people. The forty-hour work week was created by Henry Ford. Horace Mann created much of what we know as the American school system. Even the current mortgage system we operate by is a new concept created in the early 1900s. Before that time, mortgages required 50% down and were only five-year terms. These are just a few examples of "normal" life you've probably accepted without asking if it's what you actually want. We may succumb to the rules others have laid before us, but we rarely take the time to question them. I mean really question.

True vision happens when we dream—knowing we have the ability to reach our dream because we're created in the image of God.

What rules to the game of life have you accepted?

Where have you stopped envisioning like a child?

When we're bound by artificial rules, our childlike faith is replaced with fearfulness. As fear paralyzes us, we become the obstacle to our dreams and visions. Just like a game of "hot lava," our imaginary fears can seem real—and result in some destructive choices.

Creation of a clear vision precedes reality. Fuzzy vision equals fuzzy future.

Rules and regulations made by society makes the vision process challenging. So does our ability to think beyond what we see.

Many modern gadgets we take for granted would've sounded unimaginable twenty years ago. These extreme advances are easier to see in reverse when there is a huge creative jump. My family and I were driving home from a small group meeting and my kids asked, "Dad, did you have a tablet when you were little?"

I responded, "No, those didn't exist."

They were blown away. "Did you just have your cell phones?"

My wife and I looked at each other and laughed. We proceeded to tell them cell phones didn't exist either, and phones had to be plugged into the wall in order to work. And if that wasn't stone-age enough, there used to be "telephone booths" around town, which required inserting a quarter to call people.

Our kids thought the whole conversation was hilarious.

Whoever created the cell phone was probably an excellent hot lava player.

As we free our minds of imaginary restraints and see what may seem impossible, a world beyond what we have thought or imagined becomes clear.

The reality is, *created* people are *creative* people and will always create. All inventions come about in a similar way. A vision starts in the spaces of your mind as an idea. The more man-made rules you can strike from your mind, the freer your mind and heart will be to create in childlike faith. You'll be able to leap forward in the creative process and see new realities.

Many ideas are killed before they start because the dreamer takes a blank slate and draws boundaries, followed by more boundaries filled with more rules. Before long, a blank canvas filled with possibility becomes a prison. This is why rules and boundaries inflected on your mind by society and well-meaning friends and family are so critical to remove. Only then can we be the visionaries we were designed to be.

What prison bars have you drawn in your mind that hold you back from clearly envisioning the future you really want?

As we feel new soul-killing rules or limitations pop up around our visions and dreams, we must destroy them. We must become the whack-a-mole grand champions! When a rule or society norm stops you from dreaming, smack it back down where it came from.

When we dream about our future, a helpful timeline to focus on is about five years from now. Five years from now is enough time to see traction yet is close enough to be within reach.

What is your dream for five years from now? Start imagining. Right now.

With faith—and without trying to answer "But how?"—focus on what you're *called* toward, and write down your dreams. Use a crayon if it helps you tap into your God-given creativity. I ask only one thing: make sure your list is measurable.

*Um, Zech, you just told me to dispense with rules, and now you're giving me rules?*

Yes, you're allowed to talk back to me in this book. And in person for that matter. Feel free to pick up your mallet and whack-a-mole this rule about "measurable." But first, hear me out.

When we write down a dream that can be measured, we can see progress—or the lack thereof.

So, if your dream is to write for a living, you need to know how much money you'd like to make as a full-time writer. For example: *I want to make $40,000 per year as a writer.* This becomes a dream you can track and not a mere whimsical idea.

Take some time and pray and imagine one big, measurable, dream.

**Five years from now, I want to be:**_____
_____
_____

Once you've written down your vision, take a minute to visualize your dream.

How will you feel as you realize your dream is reality?

What will your family think and feel?

What will daily life be like?

Visualizing can feel childish, and it is. But that's the place we're trying to get back to! When we're childlike, we can see the hot lava and even see Reuben's stupid dragon.

Can you see your dream?

Can you feel it?

I hope so, because you need a clear vision. When your dream seems impossible, or when the opposition feels like Mike Tyson is punching you in the face and biting your ear, you'll need to return to these sacred spaces in your mind to get you back up and moving.

Do you have your vision written down yet?

Once you have your dream written down, break each year into a goal that leads toward the goal. This is how we start to change our vision from imaginary to reality.

With your five-year dream written down, break each year into a big boulder in the lava field of life. (That's pretty clever imagery, huh?) For example, if you have a business income goal of $40,000 per year, you might start with the inspiring amount of zero dollars in the first year. Then the second year's goal might be $5,000, the third year $10,000, the fourth year 20,000, and the fifth year $40,000.

When we break down a big dream, we can be tempted to show straight-line growth, but I've found most dreams don't unfold in a straight line. Dreams build slower in the beginning, as you gain skill, and momentum accelerates over time. Your efforts are compounded as you build year after year.

After breaking your faith vision into yearly goals, break down each goal into action steps. Action steps help focus your attention, time, and effort on specific actions.

What action step is required to hit your first yearly goal?

My goal of earning $1,000 dollars as an author in year one requires action. I need to create a book, write paid articles, or write for other venues to create revenue. I need customers! How will I market my products?

I like to work in five steps. Each year is broken down into five actions to work through, one at a time. As I accomplish each action, I look at how that action step worked for me.

Here would be my five action steps to earning $1,000 dollars a year as an author. My first action is to write on a personal blog for thirty minutes a day, five days a week, to gather an audience. The next step is to write one guest post a week to gain new readers. Third, I would develop a social media following to gain credibility. Fourth, I would need to create something to sell to my audience, so I would work on that for two hours per week. The fifth action would be to get feedback in order to serve my audience better and, in turn, make more money.

If the action step helps build my dream, I'll utilize that same action step next year. If I find the action step isn't working, I'll stop and try something else. I'm a genius like that.

Your dream must be unwavering. However, the "how we get there" will flex and bend. We become experimenters until a formula of sorts is found. Then we become intensely focused, repeating the action or moving on to the next step in the process.

It's important to honor each step of the process and not jump ahead. It can be tempting to plan actions ahead of dreaming, or figure out hurdles to overcome in year three when you're not finished working on year one. Jumping ahead, especially in your mind, can slow or stop the vision process.

Last week, my wife and I brainstormed about selling our house and buying something new. One moment, we had a plan to downsize and turn the house into a rental. The next moment, we had a plan to buy a nicer home. A few hours later, we were set to buy a beautiful property with a fixer-upper home. Lastly, we decided to stay in our current home. Days wasted on figuring out a whole lot of nothing. Or was it?

During the process to nowhere, all options were available, and nothing was filtered through the vision we had for our home and our finances. I was mentally exhausted—and that's a clue that you're on the wrong dream train.

When you try to solve problems you aren't ready to take action on, you can trick yourself into feeling like you're going somewhere, and you get really tired.

Vision first and always.

Anytime you feel yourself getting confused, stop. Stop and look at your vision and your action steps.

Where are you in the process? Are you ready to make decisions?

If you're not ready, don't argue with your wife about home purchases, just as a hypothetical example, not that this has happened to me personally.

Dream big and move consistently. This is the foundation of your dream. Only you can create it, and you must believe it. You must see your dream in your mind's eye, like you've already reached the dream.

Keep moving forward. Avoid the lava, and you'll save your family—and yourself—from a life of mediocrity.

## Guardrails and Guidelines:

What false rules have crept into your heart and mind?

_____

_____

If those rules were gone, what may be possible for your dream?

_____

_____

My imagination is held back often by _____.

When I feel this false rule pop up, I will remember that

_____ is possible for me!

## Prayer:

*God, I don't want to accept the rules and pressures from the world. I want to dream godly dreams unhindered by doubts and doubters. Unleash in me an imagination and faith like a child. Amen.*

# Chapter 6

## You Suck, I Suck, We all Suck

Wow, what an inspiring chapter title! But there's a story behind the sentiments.

Over five years ago, I felt God pressing on my heart to write. I'd been running my businesses, and my family was growing, but I had an unsettledness in my heart to start writing. This all made perfect sense since I'm terrible at spelling, sentence structure, punctuation, and the whole writing thing in general. This writing endeavor was like picking the area I was the "suckiest" at and saying, "Hey let's do more of that." At least that's how it felt.

Ideas come naturally to me because I write about what I do. However, communicating my ideas in written form, ugh! I didn't even know where to begin. So, I started a blog and told no one and shared it nowhere. I was a marketing savant.

It would take my wife Rachel, who is a teacher, an hour to correct a five-hundred-word post. It took her longer to correct my work than it did for me to write the post.

Another reason why I was the perfect person to start a blog (sarcasm) is I take criticism very personally. If someone offered the smallest critique about my writing, I'd break out my Johnny Cash music and my black suit.

When you take criticism personally, it's not the best idea to broadcast your thoughts to the World Wide Web. And especially when you mention Jesus. The mere mention of the name of Jesus makes the crazies come out of the woodwork. I don't see those words as great lyrics to sing during Sunday morning worship, but they're true. "Your Name Makes People Craaaa-zy" may be a new worship song after all.

So, since I'm bad at writing and take criticism personally, it made for a happy time in the Newman household. Oh, the memories. You can give my wife a gold star and a trip to Tahiti for dealing with this man.

Writing for months and sharing it with no one is a hard way to increase web traffic. I pleaded with God about the unfairness of this situation. He didn't see it my way.

So, I took another step of trusting and shared a post on Facebook. My excitement and nerves were at fever pitch as I waited to see how people would react to my writing.

I had so much support with my first post to Facebook. One hundred fifty-five views and a lot of blue thumbs had me flying high. The excitement of my friends and family lasted one whole post because my next post received ten views. Apparently, Facebook wasn't going to automatically launch me into writing stardom.

I constantly wanted to give up, so I decided to set some rules for myself. I decided I'd write three posts a week for six months, and then I'd check the fruit of my labor.

*Maybe this was a test from God. Maybe He was waiting to see if I'd be faithful.*

So, I wrote for hours and hours. Post after post. I knew God was working behind the scenes. I didn't know how many subscribers I had amassed, but I knew it had to be a lot. I had stepped into my dream. I felt it in the depths of my heart.

The day finally came. Six months had passed. How many people were reading my work? Probably thousands of people, but I knew I needed to lower my expectations a bit.

I was so pumped up as I typed my name and password. The browser took forever to load, but when it finally did, it revealed seven email subscribers.

What a punch to the gut!

I tried to cheer myself up. *It's not about the numbers,* I thought to myself. At least there were people allowing me to influence their lives that weren't previously. So, I clicked to see which intelligent people were reading my work.

As I read off the names of those who'd subscribed to my blog, I realized four people were related to me, two worked for me, and one went to my church.

I gave up writing a million times the following week. I didn't understand why God would do this to me. I blamed God, my wife, my friends, and my family for not providing the support I thought they should. Life was unfair. I can pout with the best of them, in case you can't tell.

Perspective is a funny thing. Looking back, I can remember the pain I felt, but I can also see how God was working. If someone would've said, "God's working," during that stage of my journey, I would've punched them in the nose—at least in my cartoon imagination.

The more you suck, the longer it takes to see your dream come to fruition. When I first began to write, I listened to podcasts about people who wrote a book in a weekend and became rich and famous. Well, I wrote a book in a week and launched it. Astonishingly, it sold less than twenty copies that month.

When we hear stories of the quick success of others, we usually don't have all the facts. We don't know their story, and we don't know their level of preparedness.

Let's refocus on you and your dream instead of focusing on the stories of others. Other people's stories can build unrealistic expectations—illusions. (Remember, unless you're Axl Rose, don't use your illusions.) Be mindful of your emotions when you listen to other people's stories. Are you encouraged or discouraged by what you allow yourself to hear? Don't allow yourself to be pulled down by negative emotions.

Cars can be tricky. The horsepower of a vehicle has nothing to do with the outside appearance of the car but describes the engine under the hood. And most of us judge a car by its exterior appearance.

Your life is no different than how most of us view cars. You have an outside that others see, but what drives your engine is unseen. For me, writing appeared to not make sense, for reasons mentioned, until I looked at it differently. I do have a core skill that drives writing, which is the most difficult to teach. I just had to work on the mechanics of writing.

What's under your hood? Don't judge your current skill by outward appearances. Look at what's underneath the dream. You have greatness inside you. No, I'm not talking about an alien that will explode out of your chest! (Thanks, Sigourney Weaver, for all those nightmares as a kid.) You have skill, ability, and talent. Most importantly, you have life experience, and you see the world differently than anyone else. Embrace your uniqueness.

As you embrace who you are and hold nothing back, you'll begin to see growth and forward progress. You won't improve or move closer to your dream by mulling it over in your mind. Yes, use your brain. Yes, think about different angles and strategies. But eventually, you'll need to take action.

Zig Ziglar said, "You don't have to be great to start, but you have to start to be great."

That quote has so much truth in it—way more truth than a motivational poster of a guy sitting on a ledge with the sunset in the background.

Be wildly unrealistic about what you're capable of, and move in that direction. Though we need to be unrealistic about where we'll end up, we need to be extremely unromantic about how long it will take.

The more you suck, the longer it takes to reach your dream. You may do a lot of free work between now and the time you check the goal off your list.

A good measurement for how long a dream will take to achieve is how much experience you have with the area. There is a learning curve in any new endeavor, and to not consider our familiarity or lack thereof in our time planning is foolish. I have enough handyman know-how to get me into trouble around my house. I did one summer of construction work in college, so I'm actually pretty much an expert by now. Okay, that's my point exactly. I'm slow and I underestimate the difficulty. I strut around hardware stores like I can remodel a kitchen in a weekend, but it takes me forever to fix a squeaky hinge. The only way I would get more accurate with the length of time, faster at the project, and more skilled, is with lots and lots of time doing that type of work.

An interesting thing can happen as we grow older: we switch from praising effort to being cynical—only praising results. An example: a baby learning to walk is praised and encouraged to keep trying. Could you imagine if a toddler fell down and we scolded him for his lack of execution? "You know son, you shouldn't even try to walk. Walking isn't in the cards for you." That would be ridiculous. Somehow, though, we have no problem telling adults when they fall down that they don't have what it takes.

Have you been told that you don't have what it takes? When we accept others' limitations, it squelches our future.

We often speak a failing finality into our future and stop ourselves from reaching the dreams in our hearts. Stop it. Stop doubting if you're able to learn and grow—and embrace the length of time it will take to fail forward and improve. If you're willing to be courageously patient and practice the aspects of your dream that you're less familiar with, then you'll see that time fixes most shortcomings.

The concept of growth and time makes sense when we chart physical growth, yet we forget the understanding of time when we start working on our dreams. Maturing isn't a quick process, and neither is the achievement of our valuable God-given dream..

Look at your past. How accurate have you been with how long it's taken to reach your goals or dreams in your past?

If you're impatient like me, you'll need to triple the time estimated to realize your dream. Your past has mile posts of completion where you can see how long things actually took compared to how long you thought it would take. These measurements will help you manage or stay realistic. Yes, you can change. Yes, you will change. But it's helpful to look at your past for clues on how to navigate your future endeavors.

Explore the crossover skills from your past and how those skills have prepared you for the future. For example, if you have business experience, how can that help you with that job you feel called to at a church? Or let's say you are a stay-at-home parent. How is that preparing you to own your own business? You have crossover skills. Identify them, and it will help you move into your dream with a little more speed. Again, knowing what's under your hood is what matters.

Time fixes so much, but it's imperative we work *with* time instead of fighting against it.

Time is your ally. Time is only difficult when we try to rush it or capture it. You have enough time; don't allow the excuse of a lack of time to ruin your dream.

In the Bible, in the book of Exodus, chapter 23, God drove the enemies of the Israelites out of the Promised Land bit by bit, year by year. The reason for the delay was the Israelites weren't ready to care for the land. The beasts of the field would become too numerous for them—and there were no hunters as skilled as Zech Newman. The Israelites needed time to grow internally so they could handle the land.

Let's be real. We want it all, and we want it now. The truth is we aren't immediately prepared to handle our dream. We grow into it. And I sometimes hate this truth. We care for what we can now, and when we're ready, we'll possess the land. Until then, we need to be faithful with the time and work we have.

I'm still working on my writing skills. I'm still working on taking criticism less personally. I'm still walking out my dream. I'm better than I used to be, but I've got a long way to go. I'm focused on living in this moment and in this part of my dream because this is where God has me now. And it's wonderful when I view it correctly. When I fight against time and God, it's awful.

If you aren't living your dream, work at it. Work hard and trust that God's not giving it all to you at once because you can't handle it all. Working on our part while trusting God with His part is a challenging task. Many times, we think we know better than God.

We need to trust God, and we also need to trust a community. Tapping into the knowledge and insight of others may help you reach your dream. No, I'm not talking about a "Wilson." That worked for Tom Hanks on an island, but I hope you have more community than a Wilson volleyball. You need insight into your skill. We often can't see our own superpower. We are blinded by our "suckiness" in an area which blinds us to our gift.

I confided in a friend a couple months ago that I never consider myself a leader, and he pointed out the hundreds of people I lead on a regular basis. He opened my eyes to a false belief I held about myself. He encouraged me and set my eyes right. I can be pretty blind, and so can you. Community brings light to blind spots.

Who do you trust to point out the super-obvious? (The positive *and* constructive.) We are blind to our faults just as we are blind to our strengths.

I was so nervous the first time I spoke in front of a couple hundred people. I prepared like crazy and poured my heart out on the stage.

My mentor was in the audience. So, after I spoke, I talked with him and he said, "Great job! I loved when you made eye contact with me." Translation: you looked down at your notes most of the time. I watched the video of my talk and realized how little I looked up.

I was nervous, and it showed. Funny, I had no clue that I wasn't looking up until I received feedback. I wouldn't have grown without those I trust speaking into my blind spots.

Gather a community to help you on your way to your dreams. Stay weird. Start now.

We're all in a process. Perfection is for losers. Choose the better path of allowing yourself to be . . . a growing version of . . . yourself.

## Guidelines and Guardrails:

What is an area of talent that needs to be developed to reach your dream?

_____

_____

Where do you tend to be too hard on yourself?

_____

_____

How can you practice your craft?

_____

_____

I am talented at _____, but I tend to be hard on myself because I struggle with _____. I will practice by _____ until I become an expert.

## Prayer:

*God, forgive me for looking at my own weakness instead of Your ability to make all things new. Give me patience with myself and patience with timing. I trust Your timing and will work on my craft so that the dream You have placed into my heart will come to pass. Amen.*

# Chapter 7

## Flossing to a Dream

I love long-distance running. Well, actually, I love to pound chips and salsa and other unhealthy foods when I'm stressed. I started running so I'm not *twice* the man I used to be.

Running isn't fun, but I do love participating in marathon races. There's something about accomplishing the goal as well as the T-shirt and medal the runners receive. I sit like Gollum admiring my medals, "My precious." Maybe I'll roll around in them when I acquire enough. Like Scrooge McDuck, I'll do the backstroke through them.

My first marathon was a disaster. I'd trained for months, and race day finally arrived. I was sick, and it was hot. It's important for me to begin this story with my excuses.

The race started, and I was off. Man, I was feeling good. Indestructible. Five miles in, I was flying. It was pretty much like watching *Chariots of Fire*. At about mile thirteen, I wasn't so much on the flying or feeling indestructible. It was more like crawling on the threshold of Hell.

At mile sixteen, my legs started to cramp so badly I started to run with straight legs. I looked more like a penguin then those *Chariots of Fire* guys, but my shoes were a lot cooler. By mile seventeen, I was walking, which was fine if the race was only seventeen miles long, but it's not. The race is 26.2 miles.

I walked the last 9.2 miles. I walked and felt like such a stud as older and older people ran by me. My favorite moment was when a seventy-five-year-old man ran by me, pushing a wheelchair with a boy who had cerebral palsy. So, yeah, I wasn't feeling so great about myself.

As I walked, I tried to figure out what had gone wrong as I dreamed about chips and salsa at the finish line. I was heartbroken to find out it was just crummy Krusteaz pancakes waiting for me.

What happened to me on my first marathon is the same thing that happens to many of us as we chase our dreams. My pace was way too fast.

As I looked at my time splits, I realized I was running almost two minutes a mile faster than how I'd trained. The excitement of the race had my blood flowing, so I charged out and used up all my energy.

The key to chasing a dream is going slowly enough so you don't burn out and make you and your family hate your dream but fast enough that you don't forget what you're doing.

Often with our dreams, we sprint so fast that within a few months, we're crying to our spouse about how life isn't fair, and how people won't support us, and all the other uplifting dinnertime banter.

We can be like a seasoned trial lawyer, with our mountains of evidence of injustice, all the while not looking at where we're going wrong with our race. My natural tendency, and probably yours, is to have an all-or-nothing approach, which leads to walking like a penguin. And nothing against penguins, but it's not a cool look.

Dreams need to start with a singular habit. Once the vision is established, we need to break down the vision into small habits that will lead to accomplishing the vision.

Right now, I'm trying to improve my physical health. (Don't worry, my emotional health is next on my list.)

What I've done in the past is sleep more, eat right, lift weights like Arnold, run marathons, and attempt fifty million other health activities. The excellent thing about my pack-it-all-in strategy is it lasts just two weeks. After two weeks, the only lifting going on is the chip going from salsa to mouth.

This time is different. I'm working on one thing: flossing.

That's how I roll, straight killer goals.

I'm writing this book and doing other things, but I'm only working on creating one new habit. Right now, I'm over fifty days into the habit of flossing, and soon I won't have to think about it again. Then, my next habit will start, which is to not look at my cell phone until after I shower every day.

Creating a new habit requires a couple of methods. First, you must tie the new habit to something solid. Flossing is tied to my bedtime routine. The cell phone will be connected to showering instead of to the moment I wake up. These may not seem like powerful goals, but you'll be jealous of my pearly whites and my stillness in the morning.

What's one "small" habit that will help you move toward your dream?

Dedicate the next sixty-six days, which is the length of time it takes to build a habit, to build one new habit. You'll be one habit closer to the dream in your heart and mind!

Habits, over time, build on each other and bring you closer to your vision—or push you further away. In fact, if you have a bad habit on autopilot, you're better off *replacing* the bad habit with a good one. This is important because it takes so much energy and focus to start something new.

Once a habit is formed, it doesn't require any self-control; you just do it. You can then turn your energy toward a new habit, while you floss like a boss.

When you form one habit, then a second, third, and so on, you harness the power of the compound effect. When you have one hundred positive habits moving you toward your vision, you can be on autopilot to the vision God has placed in your heart. And as an added bonus, you'll be a truer version of yourself.

No, this isn't a magic bullet or a speedy way of moving toward your dreams, but it's one method that actually works. After all, dreams aren't achieved by stopping before we arrive. Many people stop because they've been sprinting a marathon and end up on the side of the road with their tongue hanging outside their mouth, blaming the heat or something outside of their control.

Speed kills dreams, but so does inactivity. If you sit in a recliner, hanging out during the race, you aren't going to cross the finish line. Interestingly, you have to run a race in order to finish it. You must apply constant forward momentum by creating as many positive habits as possible.

Running a marathon at the correct pace still hurts. It still tests everything you have inside of you. You still have moments of wondering why this sounded like a good idea last month.

You'll only know if you finish.

There's no shortcut for character formation—and the hours required to develop your craft in order to reach your dreams. There are some pains we just have to go through. The key is to go through them.

When you run at the right pace, you can feel it. You're able to talk while you run and even the pain is still enjoyable. Okay, *tolerable*—you can take some pain in stride when you're focused on the right goals. This should be true when we're in pursuit of our dreams as well.

While we run the race, we should be exhibiting the fruit of the Spirit. The fruit of the Spirit is love, joy, peace, patience, kindness, goodness, faithfulness, gentleness, and self-control. When the fruit is missing, check your pace, and slow down or speed up.

One crucial piece of equipment I race with is a running app. Every mile, it tells me how fast I'm running, which allows me to know if I'm on pace or not. We have the same piece of equipment in our lives, if we choose to use it.

This mile check-in is a Sabbath, or a day of rest.

While we're side hustling toward a dream, rest is the last thing we think we need and the last thing we prioritize.

God made us to work, and work comes naturally to a lot of us, but God also made us to rest. Rest exercises our faith. On our day of rest, it reminds us that God will help bring our dream about. We have faith that God gave us enough time in six days to accomplish what He has for our lives. The Sabbath is our day to evaluate our pace from the previous week and set intention on the week ahead.

Rest days are like aid stations in a marathon, with free bananas and Gatorade, to provide essential fuel for the journey ahead. If you can't tell, part of the reason I run marathons is the "free" food and the glorious medals.

Rest is important, but we often don't know how to rest properly. We can imagine rest as vegging out in front of the TV, which would drive me bonkers if I did that all day long. If your job includes a lot of mental work, then rest for you may be working in the yard. If your job is physical, then working your brain may be the best rest for you. What's important is you know what fills you and what drains you.

On my days of rest, I try to do as little as possible of things that drain me. I'll even stop doing a task the moment I feel it shifting to a draining task. For example, yard work fills me . . . to a point. But the moment I feel the shift into "get it done," I'll save finishing for a nonrest day.

God designed us to work six days and rest one. When we break the mold of a Sabbath, we lose momentum and burn out.

Stay in the pocket of steady momentum and form a positive habit so you'll enjoy the journey and actually stay in the race.

## Guidelines and Guardrails:

What is one habit that is keeping you from your dream?

_____

_____

What is one new habit that would help you reach your dream?

_____

_____

What is one way you can rest weekly?

_____

_____

I will replace the habit of _____ with the habit of _____, so that over time I can reach my dream. In order to have energy to pursue my dream, I will _____ to rest well.

## Prayer:

*Dear God, often I focus on things outside of my control. Help me to focus my energy on one habit at a time. Help me to pick habits that honor You and break habits that dishonor You. Give me wisdom on ways that I can find rest so that I can do what You call me to do. Amen.*

# Chapter 8

# False Summits

After writing a blog for over a year, my time had finally come! This writing thing had knocked me sideways, but I finally had my big moment. My grit had paid off. Now my life would be complete. Cue Morgan Freeman's subwoofer-exploding voice. *Thunder nana nana nana nana Thunder!*

Scared but committed to action, I reached out to John Lee Dumas of Entrepreneur on Fire and asked to be on his podcast. EOFIRE, for short, is one of the largest podcasts in the world, with an audience of successful business leaders and aspiring entrepreneurs.

My writing career was new, but my business career was not. I owned and continue to own a couple of very successful pizza restaurants. My love of Ninja Turtles makes total sense.

After I emailed John, he quickly responded and said I would be a perfect fit for his show.

I called my coach with the exciting news. My coach excitedly told me when he was on John's show, he received thousands of email subscribers. He said one last thing: "Don't screw this up; this can make your online business huge!"

I tuned him out and started to imagine my life transforming. Like Jerry Maguire, I'd finally found what was going to complete me. My audience would say, "You had me at hello." Greatness was upon me. Finally, hard work and dedication had paid off—all three months of it. I wouldn't lose out on that moment.

I studied EOFIRE for months, listening to every episode and thinking through my answers.

I purchased a headset and microphone. Not only was I a writer, I was now a broadcasting superstar in the making. The day finally came. Let's just call it . . . my moment.

I was so nervous. Well, nervous was an understatement. I ran to the bathroom and puked my guts out just before the interview began. John was so polite and friendly. He asked me if I was ready. "Oh yeah, I'm great," I said, as I wiped the throw-up off my mouth. Thank goodness there was no video. Nothing says professional like a guy with puke on his face. That's me, though.

"Great, Zech, just send over your headshot, and we'll get started," John said.

"I don't have one. I can get that done, though," I gulped.

"Dude, raise your game. You're playing with the big boys now," he joked.

Ouch.

He quickly assured me it would be okay and I would be great. "Just send your headshot before the episode goes live in four months," John told me. I mean it wasn't as if I felt like a total imposter—oh, wait; yes, I did. My moment was slipping away from me. Stupid freaking head shot and stomach acid.

The interview went on even without my stellar nerves. You know what? It was awesome. At the end, John told me I rocked it. *Wow, I did it!*

It was the longest four months of my life, waiting for my episode to go live. Finally, the day came, and my podcast episode was dropping on iTunes. I decided to take the day off so I could watch the subscribers pour in. I wanted to enjoy the moment.

I woke up early in the morning so I could ride the wave of the day. As I updated my site stats, I quickly realized it wouldn't be thousands of subscribers I'd gain, maybe just hundreds. But over the next few days, my podcast moment only gained twenty-five subscribers.

*What did I do wrong?* I thought.

I became so depressed. I'd more than failed—I'd wasted a great opportunity.

I listened to a lot of Johnny Cash and wore a lot of black clothes for the next few weeks. I ate my emotions every day by gorging on chips and salsa, my guilty pleasure.

As you can imagine, my wife loved this spirited version of myself. (She also enjoys my sarcasm.) I was such a beacon of positivity. It took months to regain my mojo. Months of prayer and lots of tortilla chips.

Every dream chaser has to overcome the "false summit" test. The top of a mountain is the summit. But when you're climbing a mountain, there's often a section that appears to be the top but is only a false summit.

The test of the false summit has happened many times in my life. My expectations haven't met my reality. False summits are like an expectation of the finish line that isn't really the finish line. For me, this false summit only marked the beginning of my journey. It's where I began to experience a little traction.

When you realize you've reached a false summit, you need to do three things before you gain twenty pounds, have high blood pressure, or need to switch to baked tortilla chips.

The first and most important step in combating the false summit test is to reframe. You must reframe to remain sane. False expectations are the enemy to this challenge and usually include the idea that your dream will suddenly change from a difficult uphill climb to sunshine and rainbows.

My reframing centered around what I viewed as important. Was I concerned about transformation and growing as a communicator, or was I looking for the number of subscribers to my blog?

You can subscribe at *www.zechariahnewman.com* to make me feel better and receive free resources.

See what I did there? Salesman, smooth as butter, and you didn't even notice. Back to our program.

In reality, the disappointments are entirely self-consuming on what we were hoping to receive out of the situation. Our expectation of awesome rock bands, fog machines, and Morgan Freeman narrating our life is . . . unrealistic. Even destructive.

One guaranteed way to reframe is to focus on gratitude. I could rant about how if you make $18,000 a year, you're better off than 99% of humans, or how if you're alive, you should be grateful, but that wouldn't really help. Being grateful is a choice. You can have a good day, if you choose to. It sounds trite, but being thankful is a choice.

The reality is we expect a lot when we should be grateful. Gratitude fixes our attitude if we allow it. If we choose to focus on things that can never be taken away, we'll have an increase in gratitude and a proper view of life.

A little gratitude goes a long way. Gratitude is an expansive attitude that invades all areas of life. Gratitude can reverse the curse of unrealistic expectations.

When I rise in the morning, I mentally list five things I'm grateful for. I say them out loud and thank God for them. I choose to be grateful no matter what. The dream-chasing journey is challenging, and your family doesn't need their dream chaser moping around like they just found out Santa isn't real. (Um, you knew that, right? About Santa?)

I pray you make the choice to be grateful. My grateful list today includes fresh snow on the ground, my kids, friendships, fresh air in my lungs, and the sunrise. What are five things you're grateful for? Take a couple of minutes and write them down.

1._____
2._____
3._____
4._____
5._____

The more challenging the road, the more you'll need to focus on what you're grateful for. Make this an intentional habit to overcome the dreadful false summit.

Celebration is the next key to pass the test of false summits. The good news is, the more you focus on gratitude, the more you'll recognize areas to celebrate. If you're like me and many other dreamers, you don't take enough time to celebrate along the way.

Reaching a false summit knocks some people out and blinds others to their successes along the way. Reaching a false summit should be celebrated. No, we aren't where we thought we'd be, but we've had a win, a measure of success—even if our win moment included a little throw-up on the edge of our mouth.

All wins, no matter how small, need some celebration. There will be failure along the way. Making a big deal out of small wins can keep you moving forward. We make a big deal out of setbacks . . . why not make a big deal out of every forward step, new connection, and new thing learned?

Celebrating milestones places markers in the sand.

Just like God asked the Israelites to set up an altar of remembrance, you too can practice this type of remembrance with your family. Celebrating milestone moments is crucial for your journey, and this tradition, or altar-of-remembrance practice, can be passed on to your kids. You can look back, stand boldly, and say, "Remember the time God was faithful in a similar situation?"

Markers of remembrance are so important on your journey. They firm your resolve and help you focus on the journey instead of the destination. Destination thinking (*I'll finally be happy when . . .* ) is one of the biggest joy-sucks on the planet. Celebrate the small wins, and gain joy for the journey.

It's time to take some inventory. The last time you celebrated was? And what did you celebrate?

Date _____

What was it you celebrated?

_____

_____

_____

If it's been a while since you celebrated, maybe consider being less Scrooge-like and more like a kid celebrating Christmas. Believing in miracles helps, but not that creepy elf on the shelf. Be known as a person who celebrates everything, rather than the one who refuses to acknowledge any good.

When I experienced what I thought was my moment of fame, I did something brilliant and cool. (I hope you're picking up on the sarcasm because I'm laying it on pretty thick.) The time in between recording the podcast and when it aired, I waited. I didn't want to waste my best material on my tiny audience, so I waited to share my best material with the massive following that would appear out of this huge moment in time. Apparently, being on a great podcast enlarges your ego, at least temporarily. And since thousands of fans would soon be flocking to me, I had no need to work hard.

This isn't a smart plan, in case you're taking notes. This is the exact opposite of what one should do. Dreams and goals are a gradual process. Dream achievement is like investing money. You know what happens to people who strike it rich with one big shot?

They end up broke.

Money grows and expands with time; it has a compound effect. An initial investment can progress slowly, but over time, the money snowball explodes as it gains momentum due to compounding.

One action step after another, over an extended period time, is required to reach your dream. The more focused the work and effort, the faster the compounding effect.

When you reach a false summit, celebrate—leverage the moment—and continue to pursue your dream. Starting and stopping your actions toward your dream kills the momentum. Inaction doesn't just slow us down; it moves us backward.

Chasing a dream is like walking on a giant treadmill. There's a certain forward motion that causes us to stay in the same place. Walk above the speed set on the treadmill, and you advance. Stop moving, and you'll fall off the back. Ever fall off the back of a treadmill? It looks pretty ridiculous. (It may or may not have happened to me. I bounced up like I did it on purpose. I mean, *my friend* jumped back up like he did it on purpose.)

## Guidelines and Guardrails:

What measurement related to your dream frustrates you the most?
_____
_____

What is an action you can take that makes you feel accomplished?
_____
_____

What can you celebrate on a regular basis?
_____
_____

When I am frustrated by_____,
I will _____ instead of sitting in
my frustration. Also, I will celebrate milestones by _____
_____.

## Prayer:

*God, I get frustrated when I feel like I should be further along. Please give me perseverance to push through those moments. Help me to see the things that I can celebrate instead of the things that frustrate me. Amen.*

# Chapter 9

# Stinky Fish

The beauty of Alaska is impossible to describe. (But that won't stop me from trying.) Steep mountain peaks and an unmatched wildness draw me to this breathtaking place.

Alaskan summers are long, and the crystal-clear waters are teeming with delicious salmon. The rivers even bubble at points with salmon swimming upstream to spawn—and then die. The salmon runs draw predators of all kinds, from the famed grizzly to bald eagles, to this guy.

I've been fortunate to fish for king salmon many times, and one of my experiences stands out among the rest. During one college summer vacation, my brother and sister-in-law invited Rachel and me to drive the Alaskan highway with them. The Alaskan highway stretches from our hometown in Oregon, through the backcountry in Canada, all the way to Alaska.

Most fishing trips I'd taken were during the large king salmon runs in June; however, this trip was in September, and college wasn't starting back up until the end of the month. At that time of year, there was a different type of salmon in the streams.

We were set to rent a motor home in Anchorage and drive around exploring the wild countryside of Denali and the Kenai Fjords. This was primarily a sightseeing trip, but I couldn't help thinking about those tasty salmon. I hoped to sneak away for a few hours and fish. Often.

The trip did not disappoint. We hiked around glaciers, saw black and brown bears, and witnessed the awesome site of Denali, also known as Mount McKinley. One hiking excursion was especially memorable.

A beautiful trail wound through the forest and over streams. One stream we crossed had a little bench next to it, so we sat down to listen to the babbling brook. What a peaceful moment.

As we sat silently beside the stream, I heard random splashing—actually, a lot of splashing. I wanted to investigate, so I walked over onto a little bridge. There below me in the shallow stream were hundreds of salmon—hundreds of delicious, vibrantly-colored salmon to catch.

I didn't have a pole in my hot little hands, but I wanted some of those eye-candy fish. Suddenly, I had an idea. What if I caught them by hand?

Before I continue, I should mention I'm pretty sure the statute of limitations has passed for my crime. If you work for Alaska Fish and Game, I'm sorry.

That idea of handfishing sounded better and better in my mind as I thought about it.

I couldn't resist any longer, so I took off my shoes and socks and rolled up my jeans. I wandered down the bank and dipped one foot in the water.

The water was so cold it literally took my breath away. I did my best version of Lamaze breathing as the fish exploded around my feet.

By this time, my lookouts were sitting on the bridge while I tried to pretend like the water wasn't that cold.

I decided to imitate a grizzly bear, so I stood motionless and waited for the fish to fill back in around me. Slowly the salmon crowded in, and with catlike reflexes, I shot my right hand into the water.

Miss! I couldn't fail now. I stayed in the stream and waited for the next beauty to swim toward me.

After about fifteen minutes. I lost all feeling in my feet, which didn't help my prospects for providing a meal that night. But in my peripheral vision, I glimpsed a slow-moving Sockeye and decided to go for the ten-pound monster.

I grabbed the slimy guy, and felt it slowly . . . slip . . . out of my burly, callused grip. (Writers are known for their sandpaper-like hands.) Before I lost contact, I threw my hands toward the riverbank. The fish flew out of the water and onto the gravel bar. As the fish flopped around on the sandbar, I took a step toward the fish and . . . splash!

My frozen feet had failed me. I splashed into the glacial waters with a gasp. Now wet and frozen, I hobbled toward the fish and grabbed a rock.

With one motion, my freshly expired fish was ready for the pack out. I grabbed my catch and stuffed it into my backpack.

The moment I had my socks and shoes back on, we saw someone headed down the trail. It was a park ranger! Phew, I had concealed my prized possession just in the nick of time—like Gollum in *The Lord of The Rings*.

I avoided eye contact and started walking toward our motor home. *I wonder what Alaskan prison will be like. I wouldn't survive in prison. Would I be allowed to fish?*

Luckily for me, the park ranger didn't spot the crime scene—or suspect the criminal. We continued down the trail, slowly and painfully as my feet thawed and started to explode with burning pain. Up ahead we spotted a sign. I hoped it would show us how far we had to go to reach the trailhead.

Instead, the bright orange sign read: "Beware of Grizzly Bear."

Oh, great! Nothing like walking through grizzly country with a smelly, ten-pound fish strapped to my back. My companions sized me up, calculating the weight of my backpack, my semi-defrosted feet, and how quickly they could outrun me. I was sure God was getting back at this disobedient child. *This is how Zechariah Newman comes to an end, like a Grizzly-sized piece of sushi.*

But I'd sacrificed too much to abandon my prize. So we kept going, one suicidal step at a time.

After an eternity of walking, we were back in the parking lot and in the motor home. As we drove off, we were tempted to squeal the tires and speed off like bank robbers. Instead, we maintained normalcy and made it out of there with clammy palms and rapidly thumping hearts.

Now we had another problem. Where was I going to clean the fish? I couldn't do it in the motor home because it would smell the ride up—with the smell of guilt.

After a few miles, we saw a rest area and pulled over. I snuck into one of the port-a-potties, closed the door behind me, and pulled the fish out of the bag. Yep, I cleaned the fish in the port-a-potty and threw the head and guts down the toilet. My hands and forearms were covered with blood.

As I turned around to exit, the door flew open.

There I stood, bloody and guilt ridden. The shocked man who opened the unlocked door stared at me and uttered the words, "Umm, excuse me." I'm not the smoothest of criminals (like I needed to write that line). He probably thought he'd walked in on a homicide.

I ran to the motor home and implored my accomplices to leave quickly. My guilt was stronger than the smell of salmon—and I literally had blood on my hands. After we drove for an hour and a half, we pulled into a campsite for the night. We cooked the fish and dug in. With great anticipation, I took a bite.

Wow! It tasted so bad. And I don't think it was the guilt talking. It was like the Holy Spirit suddenly made an amazing fish taste awful. But as I thought about the adventure, it finally hit me. We tried to eat a salmon that had spawned and was already half dead. That's why it tasted so bad.

Turns out, dying flesh doesn't taste great. (Note to self: add that tip to my future Alaskan guidebook.) I vowed to God that I'd never hand-fish illegally again if He allowed me to not get caught—or barf. Yeah, I make big promises to Yahweh.

There will be moments in any dream-chasing journey where you'll be tempted to lie, to cheat, to break the law, or to simply overexaggerate the size of that ten-pound fish.

Temptation always starts the same way: with a single thought.

The more time we give to a wrong thought, the more the wrong thought starts to makes sense. And we compromise our integrity.

We fixate on the temptation and convince ourselves we need the salmon. We may even be convinced that God wants me to have that salmon. (*Insert your desire here.*)

We take a step, then a few more. Eventually we've gone too far to turn around—or so we think—and the risk becomes greater and greater. Before we know it, we're walking in the wild with a grizzly's Happy Meal on our back.

In the age of social media, one of the biggest areas where you and I will be tempted is lying.

Inflating success beyond where you truly are seems harmless; however, it's a step down the wrong path. Taking cash and not reporting it on taxes feels justifiable because who likes the government anyway?

The temptation to compromise your beliefs with the promise that blessed success will arrive faster, or the excuse of *everyone else is doing it*, is as old as time. The path of compromising our integrity can callus our hearts and minds to the Holy Spirit saying, *Stop*.

From river poaching to law enforcement deception, to becoming a bear's snack in the woods—how many things could have happened in my fish tale?

When we chase a dream, we need to be rooted in truth and honesty. When temptation comes, one of the most helpful steps we can take is to reframe.

Reframe to remain in the right path.

The more you desire something, the more you need to step back and look at the situation in the right light. Framing your story in the glow of a great desire can make you stupid. Reframing can wake up your wisdom.

I'm reminded of the story of two brothers named Jacob and Esau. Esau, the oldest brother, was super hungry when he came back emptyhanded from his hunting trip. Crafty Jacob was cooking up some rockin' soup, apparently, because Esau ended up trading his birthright to his brother for the soup.

The birthright assigned to the oldest was a double portion of inheritance, as well as a bunch of other cool benefits. Esau gave up so much for soup because his desire for it blinded him to what was truly at stake. His "stupid alarm" was going off, but he listened to his growling stomach instead.

You and I can be as silly as Esau. We've all done foolish and sometimes shameful things in a moment of great desire. On your dream-chasing journey, and when you're tempted to move from honesty just a smidge, stop and ask yourself, *Am I being 100?*

*What am I actually giving up by cheating, lying, or breaking the law?*

At the very least, we give up our peace when we give up our integrity.

Peace is worth way more than we often value it. That's because peace is one area we notice more when we don't have it. Don't give up even a little peace by telling a white lie; it's not worth it.

Dreamers who run the race with integrity are like the tortoise in the tale, *The Tortoise and the Hare*. It feels like it will take you longer than the fast-trackers to reach success, but that's not true. Plus, you'll sleep better when you get there.

Not only do we give up peace when we compromise, but also someone is always watching. No, I'm not talking about St. Nick. Your kids are always watching, and as the age-old adage goes, more is caught than taught. Are we, as dream chasers, modeling a race we want our kids to run? If not, we need to change the way we run and move on with integrity.

I believe you have good intentions. (I mean, you've read this many chapters, and you're still with me!) My Alaska intentions were good, too—in a fishy sort of way. For years, I dreamed of catching one of those salmon. (I did.) I wanted to provide a memorable meal for my wife and friends. (Yeah, it was memorable—for all the wrong reasons.)

If you've developed the habit of dishonesty, it's time to stop. Talk to those you need to apologize to, and turn from your behavior.

Being honest is painful at first, but this is the time. This is the time to stop. Don't entangle yourself in the web of lies any longer.

Seek relationships with people who value integrity and honesty. No one is perfect, so avoid the stinky fish who look like they have it all together but are really half dead. You'll need good relationships as you walk back to the path of light and truth.

We can wonder if we're off of the road of integrity, and a good measurement for this is if we're hiding. I avoided eye contact with the ranger because I was ashamed. Dishonesty grows in the shadows—just like fear and any other evil. If you're hiding, it's just like me hiding the stinky fish in my bag. Get rid of the stink by repenting.

If you're running a race of integrity now, awesome!

Don't grab the fish; it stinks anyway.

## Guidelines and Guardrails:

Where are you tempted to sacrifice your integrity for your dream?
_____
_____

What are the potential costs if you give in to those desires?
_____
_____

Who can be an accountability partner who'll let you know when you are having a lapse in integrity?
_____
_____

I am tempted to_____,
but I will stand firm in my resolve to be a person of integrity because it's not worth the price of _____.
I know that I can be blind to my faults, so I will make sure to have regular accountability check-ins with _____.

## Prayer:

*Dear God, often I am tempted to grab that fish. Forgive me for giving in to impulse and desire instead of standing firm in truth and honesty. I know that I will be tempted in the future. Help me to reframe in such a way that I honor You with my actions and my words. Amen.*

# Chapter 10

# Lone Wolf

A few years ago, we bought a new home. We were so excited to move out to the country and leave the hustle and bustle of town behind.

We told our church home-group that we met with weekly about the purchase and upcoming move, and the members were very excited for us. "Tell us when you're moving so we can help you guys!"

"Of course I will," I responded. But I knew I wouldn't let them help.

I moved every piece of furniture myself. In fact, the night of the move, I found myself all alone in the back of a U-Haul at one in the morning—sore and miserable.

*But I'm a man, and I don't need help.*

I would never say that out loud, but that's the attitude I often carry. Somehow, in the recesses of my brain, it honors my masculinity to do things on my own. In other words, it's an honor to be a stubborn-headed mule who's too proud to accept help from others, even when they're offering.

The next week at our small-group meeting, someone asked when we were moving. I let them know we already moved. "Great, who helped you?" he responded.

"I just did it on my own; I didn't want to be a bother."

My friends were pretty upset with me for robbing them of their "opportunity to be a blessing" as they put it. I just didn't want to inconvenience anyone. Sound familiar?

Many of us wander through this life with a tough exterior, trying to do everything on our own. Technology has made this act even easier because with a few clicks, we can be an apprentice carpenter, plumber, or electrician. Heck, we even have map apps so we never have to ask for directions again! Not that I would ask anyway.

But when you're chasing a dream, you can't do it on your own. Successfully, anyway. And on time.

You must build a team on the way to your dream. Your dream will come to fruition faster, easier, and be more enjoyable with a team by your side. But I get it. You want to be able to do it on your own. It feels safer to isolate. It feels too risky to put yourself out there and share your dream with others—because it *is* risky. But you can't do it on your own. And relationships are more than a help; they're the centerpiece to reaching your dreams.

The first set of relationships to focus on, and by far the most important, is your family. Family can be easily forgotten by the rookie dream chaser.

Your family isn't a roadblock to overcome in order to reach your dream. If you view your family as an obstacle, anger and resentment will grow and seep out. No one wants to be seeped on with contempt. They want to be cherished in love.

How do we cherish our family? We cherish our family when we include them in the dream-chasing journey. Yes, Han Solo—this is a team event.

The value of our family is something we can easily lose sight of when we fixate on a goal that's yet to be realized. It's pretty sad how quickly I can resent my family and treat them as rubbish instead of cherishing them above my dream. And it's frighteningly easy to justify this attitude with the excuse of "I'm doing this for them!"

If you could have your dream or your family, which would you choose? Yes, you can have both, but it's an important question to ask yourself. Remember when you get frustrated with your family that you'd choose them over your dream, every time.

On the way to our dreams, we'll have many opportunities to show that we value our family above our goals. Often our actions aren't congruent with our beliefs. Sometimes you'll make the wrong choice, and that's okay on occasion. You aren't perfect. When you get out of alignment, take a moment to think about how much you care for your spouse and children. Then listen to them, apologize, and change your actions.

When you value your family, you'll find out they aren't a barrier in your path. They're with you along the way. Your family helps in multiple ways. Possibly the biggest way they help is by giving you the drive to reach your dreams.

I started to write when my oldest daughter was born. Her birth, and writing, helped me think about life in a different way. I wanted to set an example for her. I wanted more freedom to spend time with my wife and children. I'm driven, in large part, to be a better man for my tribe.

If your dreams, your five-year goals, and your plan to get there don't include family, it's time to wake up and smell the salmon.

Your family can help drive your dream when you view them in the proper light. Family will also bring much-needed balance. I'm a worker. I'd work every day if I didn't have my wife around to remind me to rest and enjoy life. She balances me out.

My kids remind me to play. When my son hollers, "Get him!" and attacks me with his Nerf guns, it brings out a playfulness in me that I wouldn't have time for if he wasn't around, bringing me back to my childlike self.

Your family is the strength and weight that balance the scales of your weakness. Your family also has strengths you don't possess. How can those strengths help your dream?

My wife has helped me brainstorm stories for this book. My youngest has told me I'm funny, and it's given me the confidence to write in my tone of voice, as cheesy as some may find me.

What gifts does your awesome family have? And could it be possible your dream and their dreams unite in ways you haven't yet imagined?

Friendships are another key relationship in your dream team. Friends can be a lifeline of encouragement. They can speak into circumstances when no one else can or will. That is, *if* you share your dream with them and your challenges with them.

My wife loves me, and she has to think I'm pretty awesome. I need to hear that from her. And I don't mind asking her to tell me how super cool I am. However, sometimes I need to hear that from other people who aren't required to love me. (Rachel, if you're reading this, remember you have to love me.)

A friend's word of encouragement can keep you going when you want to quit. Friends can also call you out when you're being an idiot. I know you never do stupid things like I do. But just in case, you need to have a community that's willing to say, "Knock it off." Solid friendships are the guardrails on the winding road to your dream.

The next stage of team-building is intentionally connecting with a group of people who have skills you don't possess. You'll need people who know things you don't. Like an accountant to deal with the KGB, er, I mean the IRS.

When I opened my second restaurant, I knew I couldn't run both restaurants on my own. I was forced to hire a manager to run my first location. As the next year unfolded, a strange thing happened. My original store experienced tremendous growth.

The increase was narrowed down to one thing. The new manager ran the restaurant better than I did.

My wiring is better suited to run multiple operations, and my manager had the perfect personality to successfully manage one location. In essence, with his expertise, my company received an upgrade across the board.

What can you and only you do with excellence? What areas can you learn, and who would be a good team member to teach you?

The right people can spring your dream forward. And your dream can spring people forward toward their dream.

Mentors and coaches are relationships you'll want to invest in—if you want to reach your dreams faster and healthier. I've sought out mentors since high school, and these relationships have been key to reaching my dreams, so far. Mentors can save you from mistakes and walk with you during tough times, pointing you toward growth. Many of my mentors have become close friends.

When looking for a mentor, make sure they've succeeded in areas you want to learn about. You don't need marriage advice from your single friend. You need marriage advice from the guy who's been happily married for years and whose wife still sees him as a hero.

Successful coaches are busy. Try to meet them where they are. One of my closest friends started out as a mentor. He said he had no time in his schedule to meet with me. Instead of taking "no" for an answer, I found out he ran every morning at 5 A.M. So I asked if I could join him sometime. "Sure!" he replied.

The next morning, my alarm sounded at 4:15 am. I'm an early riser, but that was ridiculous. I rolled out of bed, managed to get dressed, and laced my shoes. The last thing I wanted to do at that hour was get out of bed, and drive, and run. But I wanted help. No, I needed help.

As each step unfolded, I slowly began to talk about personal challenges. He listened and asked more and more questions as the miles went by. As I began to share my heart, he listened and shared his. A friendship developed.

I found out later that he didn't think I would show up for that first run. We went on to run a couple of marathons together and shared many challenges and victories. I ran with him for a few years until he and his wife moved to another state. He has impacted my life more than any other mentor, and his influence continues to this day.

Connect with a mentor to teach you tips, tricks, and wisdom. But be ready to do the work. A great coach will help you with the "how" and critique your progress, but a coach won't play the game for you. (Speaking of coaches, I coach. My infomercial is in the back of the book.)

As we've discussed, your vision must be clear, so you can easily express it to yourself, to God, to your family, and to your mentors. Be prepared to verbally express your dream because you never know who could be a potential customer or who may be willing to help you with your goals.

The more you share your dream, the larger your tribe becomes. No, I don't mean constantly blasting on Facebook. I'm talking about developing relationships for relationships' sake. Don't just be a talker; be a listener. Then, when you have a need, you'll be amazed at how others are there to help you.

Dreams are built on solving needs of other people—not on your need. Too often, we are focused on what *we* want. As we shift our focus, we can build something of significance.

What problems are you solving for people?

Building relationships by listening and helping people solve their challenges will catapult your dream. If you want to open a restaurant, listen for opportunities to cook for your friends and be known for creating remarkable food. If you want to open a lawn maintenance company, start helping your friends in their yard when their time is tight. How can you be there for the people you are in relationship with, in ways that involve your dream?

Real relationships matter because we are created for connection. You need people for your dream to have meaning and purpose. You need people to help you accelerate and prosper.

And people need *you*. Your family needs you to pursue your dream and invite them on your team—every day. Others need you to help them achieve their goal. And the world needs you to realize your dream—to be an example of what's possible.

Lone wolves are lame. Join a pack, and start a movement.

## Guidelines and Guardrails:

When are you tempted the most to try to achieve your dream on your own?

_____

_____

Who can help you toward your dream?

_____

_____

Who can *you* help with your dream?

_____

_____

I'm tempted to pursue my dream on my own. Instead I will ask for help from _____, and I will try to help_____ as I see needs arise.

## Prayer:

*Dear God, I'm often tempted to go about life alone. I know that I am built for relationship, but it usually feels safer to be on my own. Help me to have eyes on other peoples' needs. Help me to see other peoples' talents. Help me to build true lasting relationships that are mutually beneficial. Amen.*

# Chapter 11

# United We Stand

Building a dream is a lot of hard work, but when you gain traction, it's so rewarding.

A few years after I was out of college, hard work was beginning to pay off. I made more and more money and felt more successful.

A great benefit of success is you're winning—and I'm a wee bit competitive. The challenge is success brings its own problems. Though I was making more money, I was also loaded with stress. The long workdays and months with no days off took its toll on me. During this time, our first daughter was born. We were already stretched to the max when we added something *easy* (sarcasm intended) like a new life into the family. This success can bring out the best in us—and the worst in us. That night would bring the latter.

After another twelve-hour, fun-filled workday, I drove home physically exhausted and emotionally beat. I finally pulled into the driveway. Sleeping in the car sounded like a pretty good option. With heavy eyes and tired feet, I walked into the house.

I had a plan. I was ready to put my feet up, hold my daughter, watch a little television, and fall asleep. A long day's work sacrificing for my family was worth it. And now I could rest.

As I opened the front door, I could hear my little girl crying. I saw my wife holding her, trying to soothe our bundle of joy, and apparently it was not going well.

"Do you know what time it is?" Rachel said sweetly. (Not exactly sweetly, but she will probably read this, and I'm no dummy.)

I thought she was asking to praise me for my hard work and dedication to the family, so I proceeded to tell her about my difficult day and how tired I was.

Surprisingly, I was wrong about her question. I'm not sure if you've had this conversation before. It doesn't end well. Complaining to your wife—who's still in her pajamas, has frizzy hair, and is holding your eardrum-shattering newborn—about how hard your day was isn't a recipe for success.

The next two hours were spent having a great "discussion" about which one of us works harder and who was most underappreciated. All I wanted to do was watch a football game and pound chips and salsa down my throat. All she wanted was sleep and an eardrum break. Both legitimate, and both requiring the other one to help. Instead, we argued until we both apologized for our exhaustion-induced stupidity and went to bed.

When you're chasing a dream, you'll be stretched. We feel this stretching the most when we're mentally and physically exhausted. I forget, and I don't want you to forget: your family is being stretched as well. You need a break from your exhaustion, but so do they.

My wife is the most graceful and merciful person I know, and even this amazing woman—when exhausted and stressed—is looking for some time off. Your family is no different. Yes, they want the dream, but they want you more!

When you chase your dream the wrong way and don't consider your family and their needs, you'll have many late-night, "philosophical" conversations that are far from productive.

Hear me, friend. The wonderful dream you envision for your family can actually tear your family apart and turn your dream into a cuss word. But when you chase a dream the right way, the pursuit can bring out the best in you and bring your family closer.

A few years and a few kids later, I had a similarly rough day as the one mentioned above. I'd worked a long day, one of many in a row. And, just for fun, a few months earlier, I had decided to take on more responsibility at work.

The stress was taking its toll on Rachel and me again. As I walked in the door, I could hear my children fighting, and then I saw my wife. She was on the verge of tears. (I know I've selected two lowlights from our interactions.) Know that she is one of the strongest humans on the planet. The key word is human, and every human hits a wall. Your superhuman partner has a wall as well.

I yelled, "Daddy's home!" As the kids ran to me, I looked into Rachel's eyes and said, "I'm sorry. It looks like you've had a rough day." After I hold her and listened to her, and after she shed a few tears, she was better, and we were better. Then I had my chips, salsa, and football.

Men, when you meet your wife's needs above your wants, she will feel cared for. When your wife has her needs met, our wants are often met. Just like my wife, your wife and your superhero has needs. What could have been a rerun of an epic cage fight became a restful night for both of us—when my focus changed toward her.

A united home doesn't happen naturally. A few small but intentional details can change your home from divided to united. Unity requires communication, prioritizing, a view of inheritance, and a heart of service. We'll dive into these in more detail soon.

At the root of a healthy dream-chasing family is a heart toward each other.

The younger, dumber version of me was consumed with what happened in my day. I saw everything through my selfish-goggles and couldn't see my wife's pain, frustration, and exhaustion. Beyond that, I couldn't see that she was carrying at least half the weight of my dream and wanted to be part of a unified team. Your spouse is carrying part of your dream as well. Every single choice you make affects your house. If you work on your dream, which you should, you are using time that could have been invested in your family. Who do you think is picking up the slack?

My wife also has to listen to me go on and on about whatever dream I've been chasing at the time. Even when I annoy myself, she stays engaged and appreciates my passion and energy. *Your dream is our dream.* Do not take for granted what your spouse does and who she is.

When I fix my view and try to see the world through her eyes, my heart, actions, and attitude change. The reality is, your wife isn't at home watching soap operas, eating bonbons, taking naps, or waiting for you to arrive home so she can massage your feet and feed you grapes.

She, like you, is working her buns off for the family. Whether your wife works in the home or outside of it, she is working. When you walk in the door, take a moment to observe the moods and actions of everyone in the house.

Our home has a long gravel driveway. This driveway has been a savior of sanity in the Newman household.

When Rachel or I are having a difficult time with the noise level of the house, we take turns walking up and down our driveway. One of us stays in the house with the kids, like a sacrificial lamb, while the other walks to the end of the driveway and back. This walk does wonders for our spirits.

How can you find moments of peace for yourself and your wife?

Creating moments of calmness for each other helps you move toward your dream. When we don't have moments of silence and the removal of pressure, we'll want to give up on our dream. Our spouse is no different.

When life is overwhelming, we get overwhelmed. Yes, you can Tweet that because it's genius. When we're overwhelmed, we look for areas to cut. I can tell you from experience, when we arrive at this point, we aren't clear-headed surgeons with scalpels. We use the "kill first and ask questions later" method. We hack with a machete, and our dream is the first area to get whacked.

Your dream becomes a point of contention because you're trying so hard to protect your little baby dream. Your family is trying to protect their sanity.

Instead of pulling out the machete and doing your best version of a jungle explorer whacking at the overgrown foliage, stop, and find your calm. Our role as a husband doesn't change. Our role is to love our wives the way Christ loved the church and gave His life for her.

That's an amazingly high standard, but it's also amazingly doable. We are to emulate the sacrificial love Jesus walked with on this earth. If this is daunting to you, you're not alone. It's daunting to me, too.

Loving your wife well includes chasing your dreams. A man chasing his dreams is alive and is a warrior for his family. Just like Jesus had a mission on earth and lived it out, you're called to live out your mission.

As a man, you're called to pursue your mission in the same manner as Jesus. Jesus always put people first on His way to fulfilling what He was called to do. When you look at the life and words of Jesus, you'll see someone who focused on the people around Him and somehow managed to fulfill a world-changing mission.

You must pursue your dreams with passion and focus. However, at times, you'll need to set your dream aside and be present with your loved ones.

In the book, *Boundaries*, Henry Cloud describes how in marriage there are areas that are yours, mine, and ours. Essentially, some areas are yours to carry in marriage, others are your wife's, and some areas are both your responsibility.

Your dream is yours to carry, but some aspects your spouse will need to carry, and some areas require both of you. That's why we need to pursue our dreams with our partner in life and not separate from them.

As I write this book, the writing is mine to carry. My wife isn't going to write it for me; however, she has made this book better in more ways than you'll ever know. And maybe we'll coauthor a book together someday.

She's also made our family better in more ways than I'll ever know. One area we do together is raising our children. I don't get to check out of that responsibility no matter what dream I'm chasing.

What is "yours, mine, and ours," in your marriage? It can be scary to address this question with your spouse—especially if your communication has been out of whack for a while. So, before you deep-dive into questions of your dream, and "yours, mine, and ours," get your head on straight. Start listening, watching, and taking action that shows you care more about the people in your life than the dream in your imagination.

When you pursue your dream in a united way, you'll not only move toward your dream faster—you'll also be able to enjoy what really matters.

Teamwork always makes the dream work.

## Guidelines and Guardrails:

What does your spouse do that helps your dream? (Really think about all she carries.)

_____

_____

When are you the most self-focused? (That's a clever way of saying "selfish.")

_____

_____

What will remind you to stop being an idiot and start looking at your wife's needs?

_____

_____

My spouse is so awesome and does _____, so that I can pursue our dream. When I get self-focused, I will _____, so that I can be the partner I'm called to be.

## Prayer:

*God, I know that unity is required in my marriage. Forgive me for thinking about myself over my spouse. Help me to consider her wants and dreams every day. Help me to courageously love. Unify my marriage while we chase a dream. Amen.*

# Chapter 12

# Communication

When I lead a team, they always end up feeling like family. I figured out pretty quickly that these people needed to genuinely care about me to care about the goals I set. The only way to create a caring environment was to genuinely care about my team.

Most of my team members, whom I have been fortunate enough to lead, were kids—around sixteen or seventeen years old. I'd be able to work with them for two years of high school and—if they continued their education at the local community college—they could be part of the team for a few more years.

What began as a managing strategy became what I loved most about operating as a leader. One team member, whom we'll refer to as Stacey, started working with us when she was fifteen. Stacey flourished in various roles and grew as a leader. She was stubborn and slow to trust (which are not necessarily bad qualities), and over time, she became an excellent supervisor.

I challenged her, listened to her problems, and encouraged her; and she became like a daughter to my wife and me. When you genuinely care for the people who work for you, they not only feel like family, but they become family. Rachel and I had a desire to see Stacey reach her full potential. After five years, she became lead supervisor.

One morning, Stacey shared her life's dream, "One of my big goals is to be a manager here." She went on to explain how this would be her life's work and would make her feel complete.

I was shocked as I listened. I couldn't help but think of all she was capable of. She could be an excellent manager but had so much more potential. I needed to raise her level of thinking. So I decided to go all "shock and awe" to make my case.

"That dream is stupid," I replied.

"What?" she shot back, waiting for me to follow up with more.

I went on to explain, "You're capable of so much more than managing. It may be a good starting point, but you have to aim for more. Something greater. You could *own* a store. Raise your level of thinking."

She began to cry.

I shared about the traits I saw in her, and how she could stretch her belief in what was possible. This would be a defining point in her life. The conversation ended as she grabbed some Kleenex and wiped her eyes. Sometimes belief—having someone believe in you—can make you cry. What a powerful and awesome moment.

I was feeling pretty pumped as I drove home. While telling my wife about the day, I bragged about my skillful conversation and pictured Stacey flying in on her private jet and visiting the store to thank me for those words of encouragement. My words would be the catalyst for change in her life. I knew it.

The next day, as I arrived at work, one of my other supervisors came over to talk to me. Maybe she'd heard about my thrilling exhortation to Stacey and hoped for her own "Zech Newman pep talk."

"What did you say to Stacey?"

I shared my speech with her, and she replied, "Actually, all Stacey came away from the conversation with was that you thought her dream was stupid."

The tears of joy caused by a mentor who believed in her were not tears of joy. They were tears of pain caused by a mentor who believed her dream was stupid. I totally misread the conversation.

She was prepared to work for my team her whole life, and I crushed her dream like Godzilla. I went back and apologized.

Unfortunately, the damage was done. She quit the company within a few months. Writing this story still hurts me deeply.

Communicating properly is crucial to reach any dream. It's crucial with the people you lead, who feel like family, and it's a necessity with actual family. It's also important to help others reach their dream.

The first thing to remember about communication is intention does not equal impact.

With every communication, there is intent. I intended to speak barrier-shattering encouragement into my employee. My impact was the death of a dream and death of trust.

When having crucial conversations about your dream, or about the stretch on family time, make sure your family understands what you're really trying to communicate. A good way to make sure the intention and impact of your communication are the same is to follow up with questions to clarify your statement.

The more follow-up questions you ask, and the more others can answer, the more clarity you'll find. In fact, Rachel and I often use the phrase, "What I hear you saying is . . ." before we respond to a question. Here's an example.

A few weeks ago, I was attempting to explain a possible twelve-month plan of attack with our finances. I was pretty excited and outlined some areas I believed we could *cut* in order to boost our investing.

In full nerd mode, I obsessed with my finance calculations. I love figuring out the future value of money. Rachel stopped me. "What I hear you saying is it's my fault we aren't investing more."

That wasn't my intent at all. She is wise and disciplined with money. And merciful. She gave me the benefit of the doubt, was honest, and presented an opportunity to clarify my communication, receive feedback, encourage each other, and get in agreement on our plan.

Making sure your spoken intention and felt impact match is the foundation for effective, dream team communications.

Unless you enjoy constantly apologizing and clarifying your intentions, study your wife and your children. Do you understand each of your family member's communication style? Are they internal or external processors? (Do they verbalize and think out loud, or quietly ponder?) At what speed does each member of your family process conversations? Do they need a lot of detail and information, or do they prefer sound bites?

I prefer to speak and hear in sound bites. Remember I'm like an A.D.D. supercharged bunny rabbit. Ain't nobody got time for that detail! If you give me too much detail, I'll stop paying attention. This has not been a winning trait for me when Rachel asks, "Did you hear what I just said?"

My wonderful bride is the opposite; she needs lots and lots of detail and is a terrific listener. When I'm talking with her, I need to slow down and share a lot of useless information. Well, to me it's useless, although to her, it's magic. For her, details make the story or plan clear. (Yeah, I know, some people are so weird, right?) When my wife shares with me, she does her best to shorten the details so I can process best.

How do you prefer to speak to others? How does your spouse want to hear? If you don't know, ask. Heck, even if you do know, take a minute to ask. Here are some questions you may want to ask:

"When we talk, do I give you too much information or not enough?"

"How can my communication skills improve?"

"Do you feel like I really listen to you?" (Top Tip for men: really pay attention to the answer on this one, okay?)

As you go through stress (building a dream is stressful), the pressure produces good—like wine through a winepress—or bad—like when your tortilla chip bag gets crushed and your chips become too small to be dipped in salsa. Oh, the humanity!

Discussing and understanding the questions above can set a powerful tone in your conversation no matter which family member you ask. But here's the key as you listen, especially in challenging conversations: do not be defensive in your responses. You asked, remember? Most likely, you have some room to grow as a communicator, and honest feedback is the answer to your prayers, whether they feel like it or not. We're all wired differently with different communication styles and needs.

For example, Communication *style* is important, but so is the *speed* at which you and your family process discussions, questions, challenges, and new ideas. How long does it take to come up with your best ideas and thoughts? How about for others in your family? The longer it takes someone to process, the more time you should give them.

I'm a much faster information processor than my wife (please note I used the word "faster" not "better"), and if I try to force her into an answer, she'll say "no" every time. Often those who process faster can "bully" the slower processor, whether it's on purpose or not.

Slower processors need space and time. Faster processors need patience.

The speed at which you and your spouse process matters because if you truly want your spouse in partnership with you toward your dream, you need her true feelings and complete thoughts. Those insights will only come out when she has time to process, share, and be heard.

Are you the slower or faster processor in the relationship? Again, one style is not better than another. Instead of frustration, your differences can be combined for wisdom. Slower processors can communicate that they need time to pray about the decision, and actually pray about it. Faster processors would do well to follow this practice. Just sayin.'

Understanding and respecting processing speed is an important element in honest communication, but so is knowing whether you and your spouse are external or internal processors. Surprise! My wife and I are different. I'm an external processor, and my wife is an internal processor. When I'm sorting through information, I use a lot of words to share what I think or feel in the moment. My wife doesn't say much until she knows what she truly thinks or feels.

Early in our marriage, I misinterpreted her silence in many ways. But I've come to appreciate her processing style. Besides, it gives me more time to talk!

Are you an internal or external processor? And what about your family members? It's crucial for you and your wife to know how you're wired for communication, so you can celebrate your differences instead of being frustrated by them.

My wife needs me to offer this disclaimer: "I am thinking out loud right now." I need her to say, "Let me think about it." Know what *you* need for better communication, and know what everyone in your family needs.

If you are an "out loud" processor, your tendency will be to talk about your dream, a lot. This can be tiring for whoever plays a more supportive role. Make sure you don't obsessively talk about the dream, so it doesn't become a recurring nightmare. "Here he goes again!"

If you're an internal processor, make sure you let your wife know about the thoughts rolling around in your head, even if they're not complete. If it makes you feel better, tell her, "This is just a thought." You don't need a complete, twelve-point plan before you share about what's up in your cranium.

Do you and your spouse have recurring arguments and certain topics that always seem unnecessarily stressful? Working through the questions in this chapter can help eliminate them. Wouldn't that be amazing?

Lots of fresh communication breathes life into the family dream.

It's not a matter of perfection; it's a matter of unity. Communication is fundamental to your journey when you chase a dream as a family.

## Guidelines and Guardrails:

What is your communication style? (Verbal or internal processor? Slower or faster process speed? Many details or few?)

_____

_____

What is your spouse's communication style? (Verbal or internal processor? Slower or faster process speed? Lots of details or few?)

_____

_____

Based on what I know about me and my spouse, I will work to communicate in the way my spouse can hear and receive the best. I will remember to communicate (less/more) in a (thorough/simple) way, and allow my spouse the time she needs to process new ideas.

## Prayer:

*Dear God, thank you for giving me my spouse. Help me to love her well by communicating in the way that she needs. Help me to remember her differences and celebrate them instead of being annoyed by those differences. Amen.*

# Chapter 13

# Hideaway Beach

My wife and I were married in 2004, and like many couples, we celebrated by going on a honeymoon. We decided on visiting Kauai, one of the Hawaiian islands. My wife loves tropical places, and I love to snorkel, so it was a great destination to begin our life together.

We purchased a book about hidden gems on the island, and we were not disappointed by the discoveries the book helped us find. But one spot in particular caught our attention. The book labeled it "Hideaway Beach." We searched for the unmarked trailhead around some tennis courts, about a hundred feet above the ocean. Eventually we found the little dirt path.

As we made our way down the trail, we came to a point where you could see the beautiful turquoise water below, but the path became incredibly steep. Fortunately, there was a stretch of rope secured to a nearby tree. Some locals had secured the rope with knots spaced out down the length of the rope to allow us to shimmy our way down.

If you've never climbed down a steep bank in flip-flops, you know that it's incredibly challenging, and I don't recommend it. Especially on your honeymoon. I'm sure I looked like Rico Suave stumbling all over myself while trying to look macho for my lady.

Finally, after our rocky descent, we reached a white, sandy beach next to the bright blue ocean. This elusive stretch of coastline was spectacular. A large mangrove tree provided some shade, so we claimed it for the afternoon. With no one else around, this was truly paradise.

Rachel decided to read a book and take a nap while I snorkeled. "Don't you want to put on sunscreen first?" she purred.

"I will after I snorkel for a little while," I chirped. (Yeah, we chirped and purred a lot that week.)

I waded into the water, in full snorkel-warrior gear, and splashed in. It took approximately one second to spot my first school of brightly colored tropical fish. There were so many fish of so many varieties that I was mesmerized.

Then, some sea turtles caught my attention, and I followed them as they swam along. The reef below me didn't go deeper than ten to fifteen feet, which gave me great comfort. I don't know about you, but when I can't see the bottom, I start to imagine *Jaws* rising from the murky depths.

After a while, I became very conscious of my tired arms and legs. *Man, I must be in worse shape than I thought.* That wouldn't be the first or last time I had that realization of not being as yoked as I thought I was.

It was time to head back to shore, so I decided to peer above the water to get my bearings. Cue the *Jaws* soundtrack. I couldn't believe my eyes. I was at least a mile and a half away from the shore.

I set out to swim back and realized the current was working against me. I swam toward Hideaway Beach, slowly and steadily, but my strength was being sapped. After what felt like an eternity, I finally reached the shore. I stumbled over to Rachel, sat down, and used my towel to wipe the fear off my face.

As I glanced at my watch, a new fear gripped me. I'd been gone for two hours. Caught up in fish and sea turtle chasing, I'd totally lost track of time. But I still had time to regret the choice of putting sunscreen on "later." My back looked like a red cherry tomato, and the next day, every movement sent lightning bolts across my skin.

When you chase your dream with your family, don't be like snorkeling Zechariah.

You, like I did, can get caught up in the beauty of chasing. You may end up wandering further away from the beach than you ever intended. This happens when a dream chaser isn't living with clear priorities.

Remembering a priority keeps you close to the beach. It keeps you aware of how many hours you've been putting into the dream. The priorities outlined in the Bible for successful dream-chasing are the same for every man: God first, wife second, kids third, and your dream last. (Sunscreen fits in there somewhere, too.) If you live in this manner, your dream team (family) will be happy, and your dream will be successful.

If you chase a dream outside of this order, you may achieve the dream but lose everything else in the process. We need anchor points so we know when the current of life is pulling us off course.

First, we need people to help keep us accountable. Your family are those people. They let you know, verbally and nonverbally, when your priorities are in line and when they're not. Are you listening?

It's also important to include voices of accountability who aren't related to you. Sometimes people who are not related to us are easier to hear because they bring an outside perspective. They are also not as emotionally involved, which makes for good accountability. Inviting wise people to ask tough questions is important to a healthy, dream-chasing family.

Here are a few questions to avoid painful drifting:

To your wife: "Do you feel loved by me? Do I spend enough time with you? Do you feel like I value you more than my dream?"

To your kids: "Does Daddy play with you enough? Do you know I love you? Why? What is something you want to do alone with me?"

If you fall short on any of their answers, ask them how you can fix it. You may find they need something from you, or need you to explain what's going on.

It's important to check defensiveness at the door when you ask these questions, or your family won't be honest with you. I struggle with being defensive but am always pleasantly surprised at how understanding my family is when I keep the lines of communication open, ask real questions, and listen. Remember that the goal of these questions is so we can be better at keeping first things first, not to score a 100% success rate on these questions. We can always improve in loving our family well, and improvement is what we are searching for.

Another way to avoid drift is to keep track of time. Anchor your priorities with a calendar. We schedule appointments with strangers and wouldn't dream of being a no-show. Yet we often forget to plan appointments with our families. Scheduling appointments with your wife and children helps keep you from drifting. Appointments on the calendar show importance and show purpose, so time and impact are both accomplished. This will help you have quality *and* quantity with what truly matters most.

And yes, you need a schedule to work on your dream. If you don't, days, then months, and sometimes years will fly by without progress. I have specific times set aside each day to work on my dream. This allows me to stay focused on my dream during that time and stay focused on my family the rest of the time. Don't be that guy who's thinking about his family when he's working and thinking about work when he's with family.

Date nights with your wife are crucial. Date nights remind you to pursue your wife while you are pursuing your dream. It reminds you that you have a partner, and it makes sure that you have a happy wife when you reach your dream. This is one way you can continually remind your wife that you love and value her. Remember to schedule these date nights and to think ahead of time what you are going to do to have the most impact on your wife's "love meter."

We have a family fun night on Fridays, which has similar impact of date nights except this brings the whole family together.

Your dream is a powerful pull often, and family fun nights draw your attention back to what matters more. Play a board game, go bowling, fishing, watch a movie, roast marshmallows, and talk about life. Whatever you do, make sure that you are engaged and off your phone.

Once a month, I have a day with each of our kids, individually. These days show them their importance on an individual basis. Each one of my three awesome kids gets treated in a special manner on these days and gets to choose what we do. These daddy dates become memorable moments of connection.

When I calendar these activities and act on them, I don't drift away from my family having priority over my dream. They also know that I care for and love them more than my ambitious dream.

What are some activities that are important to you and your family? They are worth scheduling. Calendaring allows you to have quantity *and* quality time. Quantity and quality are both important. When your family has a thriving and growing relationship with you, they get excited about your dream instead of resentful of the time and energy you spend on it.

Another aspect of being fully engaged and avoiding drift is to monitor your energy level. A few years back, I really poured in the hours at work. I would write from five in the morning to nine in the morning. Then, I'd work at the restaurant from ten in the morning to seven in the evening. The grueling weeks eventually got the best of me.

I knew my family needed me to reconnect with them. So, we planned some time away. I was so excited about the trip but thought I needed to get ahead of schedule in order to justify the time away from work. Don't judge me. You've done the same thing, right? I worked even longer hours to get ahead so I could get away.

Our departure date finally arrived, and we headed off to reconnect. I knew it was what my family and I needed.

I slept and was mostly silent the whole trip. When there's nothing in the tank, there's nothing to give your family. Monitoring your energy level may mean you stop working at times so you don't become a piece of driftwood.

Monitoring your energy level will help you, but you should aim to raise your overall energy. To have more energy, try get more sleep, eat less sugar, and drink less alcohol. (The jury is out on chips and salsa. And pizza.) Exercise will help increase your energy and allow for time to process ideas and plans. You don't need to accept your current energy level, but you should work within the energy you have *today*.

Choices become difficult when two good things run into each other. An opportunity cost is what we give up to do certain activities. Make sure you don't give up what can't be fixed.

Snorkeling is great—when you know where you are, keep your priorities clear, and plan your time. Don't let the current drag you out to sea.

## Guidelines and Guardrails:

How can you make your family feel cared for—above your dream?

_____

_____

What recurring family moments need to be on your calendar?

_____

_____

How will you be accountable to that?

_____

_____

I will run a race that makes my family feel loved by calendaring these important activities:

_____.

I will check in with my accountability partner once a month in order to catch any drift that might occur.

## Prayer:

*God, thank You for all that you have entrusted me with. Help me to keep my priorities in line. Help me to run a race that honors You and my family. Give me eyes to see when I drift out of priority and help me to get back on track right away. Amen.*

# Chapter 14

# A True Warrior

My dreams stay pure for about five seconds. It doesn't take long to veer off course with all the junk in my mind.

Regardless of the dream, I quickly became frustrated by how little my family supported me in the pursuit of my dream . . . er, I mean *our* dream. And that was the problem. "Our dream" was chased like it was only *my* dream. I'm ashamed to admit it, but I was actually living and working like I was single. As if that family photo on my desk came with the frame.

Have you ever fallen into this trap?

Whether it was the dream of owning restaurants; being a coach, a speaker, or writer; or any other idea in my heart and mind, I've struggled to put the pursuit in the right context. Instead of a vision that served others, I actually dreamed—and expected—others to serve me. *After all, I was doing this for my family!*

We all can have mixed motives. The key is to remind ourselves of the pure and good motives behind our vision. But how do we know what motivations are true and which to put in the trash?

Here's the test. If you're chasing a God-given dream, it's not about you.

Jesus was a servant leader and the example of any true warrior pursuing a God-given dream.

When we become frustrated and discouraged, it's a sure sign we've put the spotlight back on ourselves. It's important then to examine yourself, or ask your team, because I know you're not lone-wolfing it, right? Be honest with God and others about the frustrations in your heart and mind. God will often offend the mind to reveal the heart.

Translation: if you feel yucky, your motivation is in the ditch. ("Yucky" is a technical term around the Newman house.) Instead of gritting your teeth and fighting through the yucky, stop and find the root cause.

Where did you wander off from serving and begin to focus on yourself?

Often, a cause is an inaccurate view of what service really is. Serving means we perform duties and accomplish goals for the betterment of others. Sometimes our actions are the same, regardless of our motivation. For example, we can work "really really hard" on a project because it will bring in more money for the family . . . which will make them happier . . . right?

You and I probably begin pursuing a goal that serves others, but along the way, we drift into the land of "What about me? I'm working so hard." And let's be honest, we often inject a healthy dose of selfish motivation, whether it's martyr syndrome or the quest for kudos. Trust me: this road leads to frustration, anger, and burnout.

The servant-minded dream chaser will experience peace and joy and will have more motivation when days get hard.

The source of your motivation will be the difference between pulling out your Forever Lazy and binge watching Netflix, or choosing to work on your dream with your family.

There will be many days when you'd rather do anything but work on your goal. Serving others will propel you to grind out those days.

Your family needs you as a servant leader. Accepting this role releases the warrior inside of you—a warrior who makes no excuses and fights for his family.

Because I wish someone would have spelled this out for me years ago, here are some specific areas your family needs you to be a servant leader.

**1. Your family needs you to be healthy.**

Chasing a dream is not a form of cardio. Physical health is one of the most overlooked areas when we're in the heat of battle. Somehow, we think being healthy is selfish, which is just stupid. I know this from personal experience.

Several years ago, my wife kindly said, "You're eating a lot of chips and drinking a lot of microbrews . . . but not exercising." Her comment hit me pretty hard because, if memory serves, at the time I was in the recliner and wearing a fresh layer of chip dust on my shirt.

Was she saying I wasn't the Adonis I know I am? I set out to prove her wrong. (If you're keeping score at home, you're correct—this is not the desired heart motivation.)

The next morning, I went for a jog. I ran a quarter mile before I almost passed out, dead cold, in the middle of the street. It was a slow, sweaty (and extra salty due to the chips) walk of defeat back to the house. She was right. I was out of shape.

A taste of shame and defeat isn't as wonderful as the taste of beer and chips and salsa. As I stumbled in the front door, there was no victory speech from me, just a merciful smile from Rachel.

Fast-forward to today, and I've worked myself up to running marathons and have completed four. It's a great challenge and allows me to eat more chips.

Your health is a primary area of focus for a servant. If you aren't around, (meaning you're dead) you can't serve your family. Unless you're like Patrick Swayze in the movie, *Ghost*, you're not very helpful to the family from the grave.

But here's some good news. You don't need to run marathons in order to be physically strong. Simply find something you'll consistently do. I like marathons because I like a challenge, and I get to travel to different places with my wife.

Another perk about marathons is that I need to pay for registration in advance. I'm cheap, and the thought of that payment gets me to run on the dark, rainy days of winter in Oregon.

I'm just like every other marathon runner; within five seconds of meeting me, I'll probably tell you I run them. That's a little marathon humor. But here's the serious question.

What will give you extra motivation to pursue better health?

When you're riding in a plane, flight attendants provide a riveting speech about the exits, flotation devices, and oxygen masks. Before you help someone with their oxygen mask, you're instructed to secure your own. Taking care of your health is like securing your own oxygen mask.

## 2. Chasing your dream, in the right context, is serving your family.

Congratulations. You're reading a book about pursuing more in life, with your family, and you've made it through my questionable attempts at humor.

You're an uncommon man. A man who doesn't chase his dream is passive to this world. When you're tempted to give up, remember the dream is so much bigger than you. You can't give up because your family needs a dream chaser—because you are only fully alive when you're in pursuit.

We can lose the serving aspect and focus on ourselves, but attacking a dream the right way makes you the man your family needs. Only in your pursuit of what God has for you can your confidence be fully realized. As you serve others through chasing your God-given dream, you bring your talents and heart to the forefront. Instead of drifting passively to everyone else's dream, he is engaged in the fight for what God has for his family.

**3. Your family needs you to be a servant who has fun.**

We can get consumed by all the facets of chasing our dream and miss the fun. What a tragedy! There's a huge difference, about as wide as the Grand Canyon, between taking your dream seriously and becoming an overly serious person.

Wrestle with your kids, take your wife out on a date, schedule a family game night. There isn't a fruit of the Spirit called seriousness, but there is one called joy. Operate with a full tank of joy, and you won't pass out in the middle of the street.

A family that plays together stays tightly knit when life tries to unravel the sweater . . . of life. (Okay, that's terrible writing, but I sure had fun!)

You'll have to do a lot of nonfun things as an adult. It's up to you to add fun where you can.

**4. Your family needs you to actually do some serving.**

You might have pure motivation and a selfless heart, but you gotta do stuff. Doing laundry and cleaning bathrooms isn't all that fun most of the time, but it has its moments.

One day when I was toiling on my dream, pouring my soul into my project, I caught a glance from my wife. When I say "glance," this wasn't one of those *I caught my wife checking me out* glances. I mean *the* glance. The gaze of doom. The special glance that tells me I've screwed up. I'm sure you've seen it. It's the glance that makes you want to apologize right away even if you don't know what you've done.

Fortunately, Rachel began to explain how she'd really like my help around the house. With great wisdom and compassion, I began to pout . . . and tell her how she wasn't supporting *my* dream. It was a fun-filled evening. Hear me, Mr. Reader, sir; you are probably denser and less servant-leaderlike than you can imagine. We're almost to the end of this book. It's wake-up time!

We can fall into the selfishness trap when our dream becomes all about us and no one else's needs are considered. Everyone who has needs outside of our dream becomes a non-support.

When I cooled down, the stupid began to wear off. She was right. Again! This is a theme in our marriage.

I looked around the house and suddenly remembered how tough the week must have been for her—sick kids, big projects, and a million other challenges. I did some dishes and folded some clothes, then waited for my praise, like a puppy waiting for a "good boy."

Serving your family means doing things, but it also means anticipating needs and going the extra mile by doing things that aren't expected.

How can you help your wife have a better day? What chores can you do to surprise her?

How can you be of service to your children?

Chasing your dream is important. But many of us forget that folding the laundry, talking the family for a walk, and leading a dinnertime discussion are even more important. After all, your life—and dream—is about them, right?

These days, I do a better job of helping around the house before being asked, like an adult. I do this by using my eyeballs and common sense. Our family changed when I chose to serve. When you decide to reject selfishness, you'll eventually find out your wife loves your dream and loves you being a dreamer who takes action.

Wake up early and do household chores. Surprising your wife with a clean house and a cooked meal is the way of a warrior dream chaser.

Serving takes practice. Not only will your family appreciate this approach, but also those you dream of serving require an attitude of service. If your dream isn't succeeding, you probably need to do a better job at serving.

Serve with joy, and your dreams will happen.

## Guidelines and Guardrails:

In what areas do you currently serve your family well?

_____

_____

In what areas do you tend to become the most *self*-serving?

_____

_____

In what areas can you be a better servant leader?

_____

_____

I can be self-centered when it comes to _____.

Instead of focusing on myself, I will be the servant leader my family needs by _____.

## Prayer:

God, *I can be so selfish and self-serving. Forgive me, Lord. I know You entrusted me to serve my family. Help me to serve them with all of my heart, mind, and body. As I follow You, help me to serve with joy. Amen.*

# Chapter 15

# Future Past

In 1984, my dad, Jim, had a dream of being an entrepreneur. My father was a manager at a local A&W restaurant and hoped he would someday own his own place. With excitement, he mentioned his dream of being a business owner to his boss. His boss told him he didn't think he had the skills to accomplish the dream.

*Maybe being a business owner isn't in the cards for me*, he must have thought.

After the rejection from his boss, he thought about it and decided to move forward. He went to the bank to secure a loan. He had no luck and was rejected by several other banks. They told him he was too young and inexperienced.

He contemplated how to make himself look older in hopes of receiving a yes. Then it dawned on him. *Most men look older with facial hair!* So he quit shaving and, a few scratchy months later, approached the banks. He was denied again.

He wasn't about to give up, so he asked some family members for a loan.

My dad, the bravest and most persistent man I know, went to his father-in-law with a proposition.

He found a pizza place he thought he could turn into a money maker. My granddad, who was an awesome man, was not a visionary. He laughed and said, "Pizza! Who even eats that stuff?"

This is the point in the story where I'd quit and admit God was closing the door.

My dad went for one last Hail Mary. He went to his father and laid out his dream, which by that time, he'd turned into a real plan.

His dad, my papa, took out a second mortgage on their house and gave my parents a loan to open their first pizza restaurant when I was three years old. A year later, after buying the restaurant, my dad repaid the loan to his parents. My parents grew their location to thirteen more stores.

But the journey wasn't a walk in the park.

When I was thirteen, my parents chose to downsize to five stores, keeping the ones located closer to our home. My dad had missed too many of our sporting events and didn't want that pattern to continue.

Growing up, I always knew I was more important than their businesses. Their actions made it clear.

If you follow the advice from these pages, your kids will know they're more important than your dream.

When it comes to dreams and family, what did your parents pass down to you? Sometimes this is easier to see than what we're passing down to our kids. Think of what your parents did and how that impacted your life, both positively and negatively.

My parents, who are in their sixties, just opened a new chapter in their lives and business: a full-service restaurant. And they chose to embark on this journey when most of their friends are retiring. My mom and dad have new dreams and don't believe in full retirement. They still inspire me to chase my dreams no matter the odds.

I am who I am because of legacy. My papa and dad paved the way for this dreamer.

What traits will you pass down to your kids?

An inheritance of dream-chasing is a gift that keeps on giving. Your kids will learn more from your actions than your words.

When you say, "Family comes first," can you prove it with your calendar?

When you tell your kids, "You can do anything you set your mind to," make sure to model those words.

One of the greatest motivators in the world is to know my kids are watching my wife and me chase our dreams the right way. They see me rise early to write this book. They hear their mom and me planning, talking, listening, and agreeing. They see me fail and apologize. They've seen me struggle to trust God yet move forward and closer to Him in my weakness.

Look at your actions, and consider if you'd be proud if your kids emulated you.

Your greatest impact may not be whether you achieve the dreams in your heart and mind, but what your kids achieve because of your example.

Another way to insure legacy with your dream is by including your children in the dream-chasing journey.

I started working in my parent's business at the old age of nine. My dad worked on holidays.

Our family wanted to be with my dad, so we'd go to work with him. I'd wash dishes and fold boxes. We didn't see it as work; it was a fun experience.

I also remember visiting new locations with my dad as a child. I had the opportunity to see buildings under construction and watch my dad talk with vendors and contractors. I thought everyone's dad built things.

Letting your kids help with your dream instills a healthy work ethic, but it also opens their brains to what's possible.

You instill what your children will think is "normal." Some very risky things in my life haven't felt like risk; they felt normal. What do you want your kids to think is normal?

Teaching your kids about mindset, balance, and finances can set them up for a bright future. It's important for your kids to help and experience the good parts of your dream-chasing journey but to also experience the challenges.

I remember like it was yesterday. I was home from college and walking with my dad through a wheat field. He was crying and fearful.

The businesses were down in profit, and he didn't know what to do. I remember the pride I felt that my dad was sharing this fear with me. I felt like an equal.

He ended up fixing the stores, and watching him wrestle through the challenging times increased my faith for my own scary moments in life.

It can feel like you're protecting your kids by not sharing struggles, but it's more important to show and tell them about the ups and downs of dream-chasing, in age-appropriate ways that build faith.

For example, if finances are tight, you don't want your nine-year-old child thinking they may not have a bed to sleep in. However, telling your nine-year-old child that you sometimes struggle with doubt or that someone's words hurt you is good because it is healthy for them to hear.

Don't dream only for today. Choose to look beyond today, and your grandchildren will be dream chasers.

Your example and leadership can impact lives one hundred years from now.

Throughout this book, I've had you write down takeaways from each chapter to help provide guidelines and guardrails. These will ensure you're chasing your dream in a godly manner that ripples through time.

Circle one: Am I serving *myself* or my *family*?

Circle one: I'm focused on *today* or focused on *legacy*?

Attack your dream in a humble manner, and you won't just survive, you'll thrive in this glorious journey.

Now it's time to stop reading and start doing.

Information is useless if we don't put it into action. Move, and the path will be revealed before you. Be blessed on your journey!

## Guidelines and Guardrails:

What legacy did your parents pass down to you?

_____

_____

What legacy do you want to pass on to your children's children?

_____

_____

I am grateful that my parents passed down to me the legacy of _____. My wife and I will make sure to pass down the legacy of _____.

## Prayer:

*Dear God, I want to pass down the trait of chasing God-given dreams to my children so that they will be all that You made them to be. Cover areas where I come up short, and give me strength and courage to lead my family in such a way that my children's children will be impacted. Amen.*

# CHAPTER 16

# Write Your Own (Short) Book

Now you're going to write a book. Don't worry, it's more of a paint-by-numbers exercise than a novel.

As you look back at your guardrails, it may feel like a doctor's checkup. You may get out of balance and need to readjust. Along the journey, you'll screw up a lot. Heck, this book is basically me messing up and finding my way.

Apologize often, pray for forgiveness, and step back inside the guardrails you've established for yourself.

My dreams for my family:

_____

_____

_____

My motivation for these dreams:

_____

_____

_____

**Chapter 1**

When I am feeling fearful about _____, I will tell _____, who will give me the courage to _____.

## Chapter 2

Looking at my dream, I am (how far) _____ away, I will measure my traction by measuring _____. My eyes and mind will be on the lookout for creative solutions.

## Chapter 3

I am often tempted to hide _____ when I am _____. I will talk and confess this to _____ so that I can feel free to chase my dream.

## Chapter 4

When I focus on over my (past/future), I'm tempted to fixate on _____, which is outside of my control. Instead, I will _____ without delay.

## Chapter 5

My imagination is held back often by _____. When I feel this false rule pop up, I will remember that _____ is possible for me!

## Chapter 6

I am talented at _____, but I tend to be hard on myself because I struggle with _____. I will practice by _____ until I become an expert.

## Chapter 7

I will replace the habit of _____ with the habit of _____, so that over time I can reach my dream. In order to have energy to pursue my dream, I will _____ to rest well.

## Chapter 8

When I am frustrated by _____, I will _____ instead of sitting in my frustration. Also, I will celebrate milestones by _____.

## Chapter 9

I am tempted to_____, but I will stand firm in my resolve to be a person of integrity because it's not worth the price of _____. I know that I can be blind to my faults, so I will make sure to have regular accountability check-ins with _____.

## Chapter 10

I'm tempted to pursue my dream on my own. Instead, I will ask for help from _____, and I will try to help_____ as I see needs arise.

**Chapter 11**

My spouse is so awesome and does _____ so that I can pursue our dream. When I get self-focused, I will _____ so that I can be the partner I'm called to be.

**Chapter 12**

Based on what I know about our communication styles (verbal or internal processor, slower or faster process speed, desiring many details or few), I will work to communicate in the way my spouse can hear and receive the best. I will remember to communicate (less/more) in a (thorough/simple) way and allow my spouse the time she needs to process new ideas.

**Chapter 13**

I will run a race that makes my family feel loved by calendaring these important activities:

_____
_____.

I will check in with my accountability partner once a month in order to catch any drift that might occur.

**Chapter 14**

I can be self-centered when it comes to _____.
Instead of focusing on myself, I will be the servant leader my family needs by _____.

## Chapter 15

I am grateful that my parents passed down the legacy of
_____.

My wife and I will make sure to pass down the legacy of
_____.

Guess what I'd like you to do with this list.

That's right: schedule a time with your spouse and share your dream and what you've learned from this book, and ask about your spouse's dreams.

Schedule a time every month where you revaluate these guardrails and guidelines and have a marriage checkup. It may be a time to ask for forgiveness and have a fresh start. Pray together and unite around dreams that will bless your family.

You want to chase your dreams. But who will be with you when you arrive? A solo journey on a motorcycle might seem faster, easier, and more exciting. But trust me, when you chase a dream in a minivan full of family and friends, you'll enjoy the journey—and the destination.

Zechariah, or Zech, as many know him, is the author of this book and is a serial dreamer. From marrying his high school sweetheart, building two successful restaurants, and running small groups at a multiple-site church, to writing, coaching, and speaking, he is always on the move to bring dreams into reality.

When he isn't hanging out with his wife and three kids, you can find him running marathons, catching fish in some stream (legally), or hunting big game in the Oregon mountains and deserts.

He has written for *Fast Company*, *Entrepreneur*, and *Faith Driven Business*, and has been featured at Fox News and NBC. His passion is to help others pursue their dream in a way that brings their family closer together and builds a rock-solid foundation of faith.

*ZechariahNewman.com*

# Fuel for Chasing Your Dreams

Unless you like mice and the Forever Lazy, I want to get to know you.

I send out awesome content to keep you engaged in dream-chasing, in a healthy way, at *zechariahnewman.com*. Subscribe there, and I'll even give you free stuff to help your journey. (*Yes, I bribe people to be my friends. I know that's the gift that keeps on giving!*)

I'm an experienced speaker and accustomed to all kinds of requests—and all belief systems and needs. My speaking is just like my writing: you will hear real-life examples with heart and humor. Most of all, your audience will receive new insights and answers. Please contact me at *zechariahnewman.com/speaking*, if you need a speaker.

If you are interested in coaching, I do that, too—on a limited basis. (*Man, I'm like a Swiss Army knife and Chuck Norris in one . . .*) Email me at *zechariahnewman@gmail.com*

www.ingramcontent.com/pod-product-compliance
Lightning Source LLC
Chambersburg PA
CBHW071031240526
45469CB00006BD/2173